The
Harlot's Handbook

About the Author

Hallie Rubenhold was born in Los Angeles to English parents, studied history at the University of Massachusetts and history and the history of art at the University of Leeds where she received her MA and MPhil in eighteenth-century British social history. She is the author of the history of the List, *The Covent Garden Ladies: Pimp General Jack & the Extraordinary Story of Harris's List*, also published by Tempus. She worked as the Assistant Curator at the National Portrait Gallery, London before deciding to teach history and write full-time. She lives in Muswell Hill, London.

The
Harlot's Handbook
HARRIS'S LIST

HALLIE RUBENHOLD

TEMPUS

NOTE TO THE READER

Spellings are as they appear in the original *Harris's List*.
The names of the prostitutes are partially obscured
as they were in the original *List*.
The Editor

Cover illustrations:
Back and spine: *Frontispiece from Harris's List, 1793. Tempus Archive.*
Front: *Hogarth engraving, courtesy of Jonathan Reeve.*

This edition first published 2007

Tempus Publishing Limited
Stroud, Chalford,
Stroud, Gloucestershire, GL6 8PE
www.tempus-publishing.com

© Hallie Rubenhold, 2005, 2007

The right of Hallie Rubenhold to be identified as the Author
of this work has been asserted in accordance with the
Copyrights, Designs and Patents Act 1988.

British Library Cataloguing in Publication Data.
A catalogue record for this book is available from the British Library.

ISBN 978 07524 4384 3

Typesetting and origination by Tempus Publishing Limited
Printed in Great Britain
Internal lllustrations courtesy of Jonathan Reeve.

TABLE OF
CONTENTS.

GLOSSARY.

Bawd:	a woman who procures prostitutes.
Bawdy house:	a brothel.
Bagnio:	a bath-house, usually a location where sexual favours could be received.
Bilk:	to cheat someone out of their pay.
The Blind Boy/ Blind Visitor:	a penis.
Blood:	a 'riotous and disorderly fellow'.
Bow Street:	the headquarters of

the magistrate, John Fielding, and his flying squad, the 'Bow Street runners'.

'A brace of shiners': a handful of coins.

Bridewell: the Clerkenwell-based prison for prostitutes.

Bubbies: breasts.

Buck: a 'man of spirit' or a debauchee.

Bully: a man who acts as a protector to a prostitute, also the eighteenth-century equivalent of a bouncer.

Bunter: a destitute prostitute.

Cantharides: aphrodisiacs.

Chariot: a phaeton or two-wheeled carriage (could also be a reference to a coach).

Clap: a 'venereal taint', usually gonorrhoea.

Compter/Round House: a local lock-up or gaol.

Cull/Cully:	a prostitute's customer.
Eringoes and Electuaries:	aphrodisiacs.
Favourite:	a prostitute's best client, someone for whom she may feel genuine affection.
Flash-man:	a pimp or a bully to a bawdy house.
The Fleet:	London's main debtor's prison.
'A good piece':	a physically attractive woman.
High-keeping:	the extravagant maintenance of a prostitute in expensive lodgings.
'In keeping':	the state of being financially supported by one man as his mistress.
[The woman who] 'keeps the house':	the woman to whom a house is let, or the resident procuress.
King's Bench Prison:	the Southwark-based

	prison generally used for holding debtors and those guilty of libel.
The Lock Hospital:	a hospital for the cure of venereal disorders. Founded in 1746.
Macaroni:	a foppishly dressed gentleman.
Mantua-maker:	a dressmaker.
The Marshalsea:	a Southwark-based prison mainly used to house debtors in the eighteenth century.
Mercury:	the primary ingredient in treatments for venereal disorders.
Newgate:	London's chief prison where its most dangerous felons were held.
Panderer:	a slightly higher ranking pimp who worked within doors.
Pimp:	a man who seeks 'to bring in customers and to procure… wenches'.

Pox:	syphilis.
Queer Cull:	a customer who favours anal intercourse.
Rake:	a 'lewd debauched' man. Other terms include ranger or roué.
'A rose never blown upon':	a virgin.
Sal/ salivation/ 'down in a sal':	someone in the midst of a mercury treatment for venereal disease. Among other symptoms, the ingestion of mercury brought on profuse salivation.
Serail:	a high-class French-style brothel.
Spunging House:	a bailiff's lock-up house 'to which persons arrested are taken till they find bail, or have spent all of their money'.

A BRIEF INTRODUCTION TO THE Harris's List *of* Covent Garden Ladies;

Or HOW A POOR IRISH POET AND ENGLAND'S PIMP-GENERAL CAUS'D A SCANDAL IN PRINT

In 1757, Samuel Derrick sat with his head in his hands. From behind the heavy door of a debtor's spunging house, he had plenty of time to contemplate his catalogue of misfortunes. They had begun six years earlier when Derrick had decided to abandon his lucrative career as a Dublin linen draper and embark upon a life of excess in London. To a young man of twenty-seven, weighted with dreams and propelled by enthusiasm, the capital promised a clear path to riches and fame. He had envisioned himself as an actor, treading the boards along side David Garrick. He had imagined himself as a celebrated dramatist, penning modern classics for the stage. But above all, Derrick had pictured himself as 'a poet of the first rank', someone whose name might join those of Alexander Pope and John Dryden in the pantheon of literary greatness. But sadly, none of this was to be.

Perched on a wooden stool which rubbed against his notoriously bony frame, Derrick

was miserable. In the interceding months, the aspirant poet had managed to lose everything: his mistress, his inheritance, his possessions, and his golden dream of success. Luck, it seemed, had deserted him altogether. Ingenuity, however, had not.

It was an act of desperation, an urgent desire to escape imprisonment, that prompted Sam Derrick to scribble out his version of *The Harris's List of Covent Garden Ladies*. Unbeknownst to the impoverished hack, his lurid work was destined to become an instant sensation and the only literary triumph he was ever to enjoy. Unfortunately, his *magnum opus* was not the sort of publication about which one might boast. For the thirty-eight years (1757–1795) that *The Harris's List* rolled off the printing presses, Sam Derrick's association with it was to remain something of a secret.

Upon his arrival in London in the late 1740s, Sam Derrick's first port of call had been Covent Garden, the capital's hedonistic heart. Here, the area's most renowned watering holes pulsated with a carnival-like atmosphere. Anyone with literary, artistic or criminal inclinations was drawn to its vibrant glow. On most evenings, at its two premier establishments, the Shakespear's Head Tavern and the Bedford Coffee House, a visitor might brush their coat against that of Samuel Johnson, David Garrick, Joshua Reynolds, Samuel Foote, William Hogarth, Tobias Smollett or Henry Fielding. Hedged in by the two main theatres, Covent Garden and Drury Lane, and a mere spitting distance from Fleet Street, the Piazza bristled with actors, musicians, painters, acrobats, writers, dancers and publishers. Prostitutes were an equally visible presence, from celebrated courtesans like Fanny Murray and 'resting' actresses like Mrs. Abingdon to tavern-trawling molls and streetwalkers. Mingling, drinking, gossiping and fornicating, business and pleasure bled easily together. More than anywhere else in the capital, Covent Garden, with its eccentric mix of personalities, was a breeding ground for ideas and discussion, an incubator of creativity.

In the quest for well-heeled patrons for his proposed works of poetry, Derrick drained many a bottle with both the note-worthy and the notorious. As a passionate devotee of wine and women, his indulgence in Covent Garden's carnal pleasures threw him at the feet of the Piazza's reigning emperor of sin, Jack Harris (properly known as John Harrison). As the chief waiter at the Shakespear's Head as well as the self-proclaimed *Pimp-General of All England*, Harris carried on his person one of the most intriguing items of pimp's paraphernalia in London. It was likely to have been at the Shakespear that Derrick first encountered the work; a handwritten ledger comprised of more than 400 names of the capital's 'votaries of Venus'. Harris's list bulged with a variety of intimate details which were amended and annotated on a regular basis. Recorded beside the names of women like 'Kitty Buckley', 'Miss Smith' and 'Cherry Poll' were not only the most current addresses where they might be found, but their ages and prices, descriptions of their physical characteristics, biographical details, comments about their health and, of course, their specialised services. Although every pimp was acknowledged to have compiled some type of handwritten list, Harris's, through its sheer volume, trumped all of them. It gave him an incontestable monopoly over the area's flesh trade and, within the span of six years, an income comparable to that earned by the first Lord of the Treasury.

Harris's inventory of names not only whetted Derrick's sexual appetite, but his inspiration. Fearing his impending transfer from Bailiff Ferguson's spunging house to the horrors of the Fleet prison, Sam Derrick decided that the time was right to play his hidden card. He would create his own version of Jack Harris's list. He had witnessed firsthand how the Pimp-General swaggered through the colonnades of the Piazza, how his mighty roll-call of names had bought him jewelled buttons and silk frockcoats. If he, through the production of a similar work, could reap so much as an ounce of the gold that Harris's handwritten list had yielded, his creditors could be paid and his liberty secured. There was, however, one obstacle. Harris the pimp was not a man to trifled with. A criminal and a bully, his nefarious influence stretched from Wapping in the east to Soho in the west. There were few willing to challenge his supremacy, let alone attempt to mine from his field of wealth. Were Derrick's plan for a list of his own to prove successful, it would require a nod of approval from Jack Harris. That gesture was not likely to be granted without a substantial cash offering.

What the actual terms of the agreement were that existed between Sam Derrick and Jack Harris will never be known. It is likely that Derrick agreed to pay the pimp a one-time permission fee for the use of his name. As Georgian London's printing presses spewed forth heaps of literary slurry each week, neither Derrick not Harris would have been able to predict the success of what would have seemed initially to be a short-term venture. In later years, Harris would be haunted by his foolhardy decision, one which resulted in his exclusion from such an advantageous enterprise. A stroke of unfortunate irony meant the pimp would never be able to compete with the success of his own name. In an attempt to claw back a portion of the profits to which he felt entitled, he established his own press in 1765 and published a rival to Derrick's *Harris's List*, entitled *Kitty's Attalantis*. The work was a failure and never ran beyond one edition.

What the pimp's second-rate publication lacked was the sparkle of Sam Derrick's pen.

Derrick may not have been a skilled poet, or even an actor of discernable talent, but his ability to observe and document the nuances of his world and the assorted characters who inhabited it was indisputable. A journalist before the great age of print, Derrick recorded life in Covent Garden – the bar brawls, the pranks, the rivalries, the romances and broken hearts – and recounted them through the vehicle of his publication. While the ultimate purpose of *The Harris's List of Covent Garden Ladies* was to guide the desirous to the desirable, it served as more than simply a replica of a pimp's little black book. Years of avid womanising provided Derrick with a rich source of personal knowledge from which to draw his own compendium of names, as did the candid contributions from associates and the area's locals. The result was a witty chronicle of the Piazza's women, which included tales of their exploits, assessments of their personalities and retellings of inside jokes, all intended to raise a laugh from Covent Garden's circle of rakes. Derrick's version of *The Harris's List* was designed as much for the entertainment of the mind as it was for the loins.

Derrick's publisher, the enigmatically named H. Ranger, immediately recognised the twinkle of guineas in the author's sparky work and advanced him the funds necessary to secure his release. Within months, the first edition of *The Harris's List* was available for purchase. In 1757, any literate person of means might amble down to Covent Garden, where he could buy a copy from the Shakespear's Head, or the neighbouring brothel of Mother Jane Douglas, for two shillings and sixpence. In later years, the six-by-four-inch volume became much more widely obtainable. It could be purchased on Fleet Street, directly off H. Ranger's shelves; from the kiosk in the Piazza; and at any other number of houses of ill-repute within the vicinity. By the 1770s, H. Ranger was advertising a full range of *Harris's Lists* in the newspaper, including issues from previous years. As the popularity of the *List* grew (it is estimated to have sold 8,000 copies annually), so it also began to assume the characteristics of a standardised publication. Each year, *Harris's* enthusiasts could look forward to its reissue during the Christmas period, when:

> Again the coral berry's holly glads the eye,
> The ivy green again each window decks,
> And mistletoe, kind friend to Bassia's cause,
> Under each merry roof invites the kiss...

Unfortunately, it was the *List*'s very success that eventually became its downfall.

Until 1769, the year of his death, Sam Derrick remained the sole editor of this infamous work. It was a position that, after his election to the estimable position of Master of the Ceremonies at Bath and Tunbridge Wells in 1761, he might well have relinquished. But *The Harris's List*, and the women who featured on it, remained close to Derrick's heart. Covent Garden's ladies had been among some of his most ardent champions during his difficult days. The *List*, he felt, was not so much a tool of exploitation as an implement that provided otherwise impoverished women with an income, as well as opportunities to meet potentially generous lovers. It was for this reason that upon his death he willed the proceeds of his 'new edition of *Harris's List*' to his 'old friend and mistress, Charlotte Hayes', the courtesan whom he had always loved, but could never afford. It was only after Derrick had been laid in earth that the lid was lifted on his secret. Amid much hilarity, 'the little King of Bath' was recognised publicly as the author of the scandalous guide.

Who Sam Derrick's mysterious successors were is unknown. Like Harris the pimp, who was finally arrested in 1758, the publishers of *The Harris's List* were eventually to grow too bold, too proud, and too sloppy. By the late 1780s, the publication of the work had been assumed by two brothers, John and James Roach of Vinegar Yard, and a third conspirator, John Aitkin of Bear Street. Together, the three published a range of smut under the name of H. Ranger. However, by the time the Roaches and Aitkin had taken up the gauntlet, *The Harris's List* was becoming a slightly tired annual and a far cry from its earlier incarnation as an anthology of local characters. In an attempt to appeal to a broader readership, one which might not be familiar with Covent Garden or the topography of the West End, the *List*'s editors exchanged its quirky tales for stock seduction stories. Names and the details of their exploits became interchangeable; the joyous romps of Miss Smith were easily transformed into the debauched adventures of Miss Jones. As long as the addresses and prices were vaguely correct, no one was expected to complain.

The ensuing publishers of *The Harris's List of Covent Garden Ladies* also attempted to move with the whims of their era. As the eighteenth century progressed, notions of gentility were beginning to pervade almost every walk of life, even the most unexpected. Sex with a prostitute moved from the realm of base, grunting euphemisms to a thing of beauty. No longer described as 'squat, swarthy, round-faced' wenches, now these 'daughters of Venus' were praised for their 'fonts of pleasure' and 'moss-covered grots of love'. In the desire to clean up the *List*'s language, much of its original character was scrubbed away.

On a winter's day in January 1795, the long, twisting tale of *The Harris's List* came to an abrupt end. Shortly after the annual's reissue, the Roach brothers received a visit from the law. A group of moral reformers headed by 'A great number of Gentlemen of the Highest Rank and Estimation' had demanded the prosecution of those responsible for the publication's production. James Roach was hauled before Justice Ashurst, fined £100 and sentenced to a year in Newgate Prison. Regardless of the profitability of running filth through their printing presses, after a sobering stint in prison, neither the Roach brothers nor anyone else was prepared to risk their livelihood for the sake of Derrick's worn-out guidebook.

Once the manufacture of the *Harris's List*s had ground to a halt, it was not long before the remaining traces of its existence began to evaporate. In the relentless moral march of the nineteenth century, the sequestered copies of this reprehensible publication would have been unearthed, one by one. Discovered among more respectable texts, or hidden in drawers, squirreled in corners, boxes or locked cabinets, the majority were weeded out by clean Victorian hands and committed to the hearth's lapping flames.

The issue reproduced in this book, that from 1793, is the last surviving edition in public possession. In order to provide a flavour of earlier works, a second section has been included which draws from eight other extant volumes, those from 1761, 1764, 1773, 1774, 1779, 1788, 1789 and 1790. Few as they are in number, it is remarkable that these copies have defied the censure of the years.

Even to modern eyes, wearied by constant media titillation, *The Harris's List* makes for intriguing reading. In the twenty-first century it is often fashionable to bemoan the world we have lost, one devoid of *Big Brother* and the publicised sex stunts of celebrities. But the pages of the *Harris's List* demonstrate that we cannot search for our innocence in the era of Jane Austen, either. The spirit of eighteenth-century Covent Garden has always been with us.

Hallie Rubenhold,
Muswell Hill, London

ACKNOWLEDGEMENTS

Thanks are due to a number of people, primarily my *Pimp-General* at Tempus Publishing, Jonathan Reeve, and his second-in-command, Sophie Bradshaw. I would also like to express my gratitude to Martin Palmer at Tempus, and my patient husband Frank.

꙳꙳꙳꙳꙳꙳꙳꙳꙳꙳꙳꙳꙳꙳꙳꙳꙳꙳꙳꙳꙳꙳꙳꙳꙳꙳

HARRIS's LIST

OF

Covent Garden Ladies

OR

MAN OF PLEASURE'S KALENDER

FOR THE YEAR 1793

CONTENTS.

D

E

F

G

H

J

K

L

M

P

R

꧁꧂꧁꧂꧁꧂꧁꧂꧁꧂꧁꧂꧁꧂꧁꧂꧁꧂꧁꧂꧁꧂꧁꧂

HARRIS's LIST

OF THE

Covent Garden Ladies

———

Mifs D–vis, No. 22, *Upper Newman-street.*

Artful Ways beguile the implicit rake.

This is a fine lively girl, about twenty-one, rather above the middle size, genteelly made; has several good friends, but is much attached to young Br–om, the lottery-office-keeper, who is now in prison, where she often visits him; is ever obliging, and seldom out of humour, understands a great deal of her business, and never fails to please. She enjoys her favourite man with ecstasy; and pleases, with cold indifference, managed by art, the rest of her votaries; who are content with thinking they have fathomed the deepest part of a girl so replete with sensation; in short, she can so well counterfeit the passions of love and lust, that many of the most knowing rakes of the town would be easily deceived. This lady occupies the parlour.

Mifs Godf–y, No. 22, *Upper Newman-street*.

If parts can conquer great and small,
Sure – and Godf–y must needs do all.

This lady is a kind of boatswain in her way, and when she speaks, every word is uttered with a thundering and vociferous tone. She is a fine lively little girl, about twenty-two, very fond of dancing, has dark eyes and hair, well shaped, and an exceeding good bed-fellow, will take brandy with any one, or drink and swear, and though but little, will fight a good battle. We apprehend this lady would be an extraordinary good companion for an officer in the army, as she might save him the trouble of giving the word of command.

She resides in the first floor.

Mrs. P–ge, No. 26, *Upper Newman-ſtreet.*

Come, thou Goddess, fair and free,
With the sweet simplicity.

The above two lines are highly descriptive of Mrs. P–, who for ease, freedom and simplicity is scarcely to be matched among the whole sisterhood, besides which, her beauty is by no means inconsiderable. She is about twenty, has been near five years in business, and has had tolerable fortune; her features are good, except her mouth, which is a little too wide, especially when she laughs, which is pretty often. Those who are inclined to mirth, will find her to be a good companion, without the least tincture of blasphemy, she is not of a mercenary disposition, yet she expects one pound one, but rather than lose a customer will put up with half the sum.

Mrs. R–ad, No. 66, *Queen Anne Street East.*

With the sports of the field, here's no
      pleasure can vie,
Then follow, follow, &c. the hounds in full
      cry.

A fine tall girl, about twenty-two, elegant in person, with a captivating countenance. She has found out the true art to please and be pleased. Mrs. R–d has very dark eyes and eye-brows, and plenty of the same colour hair on the enchanting spot of love, being a fine cover for game. This lady has tasted the sweets of many good things in purse and person, and relishes them all. Her predominant passion seems for horses, hounds, and the delights of the field. No one is more emulous than our heroine, to be in at the death; upon the whole we may pronounce this lady a woman of taste and spirit, which she displays in nothing more forcibly, hunting not excepted, than in the choice of her favourite, as he is still a hunter.

Mrs. L–tle–n, No. 3, *Salisbury-ſtreet, Strand.*

——. Since we mortal lovers are,
Ask not how long our love will last;
But while it does, let us take care,
Each minute be with pleasure past.

This is a fine plump girl, with dark hair, large eyes, and dark eye-brows. It is a very great misfortune for ladies, who depend on the public for a support, to be liable to particular attachments, where interest is out of the question, for it has been of great detriment to this lady, when she has had good keepers, who have discovered her intrigues, merely through her own carelessness, and have discarded her. As her circumstances are particularly fluctuating, so her dress is answerable to them. She is, upon the whole, an agreeable woman, and we make no doubt, might live exceeding genteel, were she more guarded in her conduct, and keep herself from falling in love where there is no pecuniary view; however, at present, she is in keeping with Mr. B–, a couns–r in the Temp–e, but will not

lose the enjoyment of other friends, who may fall in her way.

Mrs. Bi–d, No. 17, *Salisbury-ſtreet, Strand.*

For 'tis vain to guess
At women by appearances;
They paint and patch their imperfections
Of intellectual complexions,
And daub their tempers o'er with washes,
As artificial as their faces.

Those who keep ladies do not seem to regard their charms, but become keepers because it is the fashion. But she cannot be admired on account of her charms, for she has very few; indeed we are so blind that we cannot discern any. She is tall and lusty, has a dead eye and flattish nose, and good teeth, and is very much given to laughing, she wears short petticoats. We do not know whether her favours are bestowed for money or love, but this we are certain of, that C– H– is not the only man who experiences the happiness of her voluptuous favours, which are very numerous.

Mifs Bro–n, No. 4, *Princess-ftreet, Cavendish-square.*

Say lovely youth would'st thou thus betray,
My easy faith and lead my heart astray.

The situation of this lady is truly pitiable, for as we understand, her heart was betrayed by a young gentleman in the country, who soon forsook her, which she repeats with a good deal of apparent grief, and does not seem at all calculated for her present way of life, except in point of beauty. Is rather short, and has a clear fair skin, with a pleasing blue eye, her cheeks are very prettily dimpled, and she has a natural fresh colour, her hair is bright, and her teeth are good. She is now a lovely desirable girl, but if she continues long in her present situation, it is a great chance but that she becomes as false inconstant and infamous as many others of the fraternity. By this remark we do not mean to anticipate any disagreeable circumstances, but mention it merely to her as a friendly caution that may possibly raise her pride and guard her against those baneful habits which are so often the disgrace and sometimes the ruin of many of the sex.

Miſs Dav–s, No. 38, *Margaret-ſtreet, Oxford Market.*

Is a fine tall young woman, of about eighteen, has a fair complexion, and excellent features; her mouth is small, and looks when closed, like a rose when it begins to bud; her eyes, however, are no great advantage to her, as they are small and gray. She has the character of a spirited, spitefully-fond bed-fellow that will keep her spark to the *mark* of business as long as he has strength to follow his *labour* with any pleasure or ability. She is seldom guilty of those vices which we have so frequently censured, and which defile the sex more than any other; we mean drinking and swearing. This, however, is not to be wondered at, when it is known, (which her company will easily discover,) that she has been excellently educated, and notwithstanding the unfortunate bent which she has taken, yet there are some of the stamina of the original virtues planted in her mind to be discovered, and which no practices will so eradicate as to render her vulgar or disagreeable.

Mifs Sc–tt, No. 44, *Margaret-ftreet, Cavendish-square.*

'Ads bobs she's wondrous pretty!
Her looks are almost jetty;
She's a finer wench then Betty,
And lo! her eyes are blue!

We cannot call this lady a beauty of the first rate; she is what may be determined pretty, but nothing extraordinary, and tho' she cannot boast of all those external graces, which distinguish the beauties of some ladies; yet I've heard, when she is engaged in her business, there are very few who are her superiors. She is amorous to the greatest degree, and has courage enough not to be afraid of the largest and the strongest man that ever drew weapon in the cause of love. She has had a number of admirers in her time, all of which she had the satisfaction of pleasing during their temporary residence with her. She is now in keeping by one Mr. B–, who is not a little enamoured of her. Her person is of the middling size, little black eyes, black hair, very fine teeth, and is altogether very agreeable.

Mifs Ke–t, No. 9, *Warren-ftreet, Tottenham Court Road.*

Round your neck, like the ivy, she'll fold her
    sweet arms,
And wickedly wanton display all her charms;
With transport she'll usher your hand to her
    breast,
Whilst with her's she applies the *tumid bold
    guest.*

Here the epicures in youth and beauty may satisfy their most ardent longings. Here Venus seems to have shed her choicest influence; and Cupid has called forth his choicest arrow of the amorous kind to warm her little breast to soft enjoyment. 'Tis not a lukewarm flame that burns in her breast, no, 'tis an enthusiastic rapture which enlightens her whole soul with the divine spirit of love. Whenever she is offering incense at the shrine of Venus, her whole frame is agitated with pleasure, her eyes languish, her breasts heave, and her limbs quiver; while involuntary sighs and murmurs burst forth from her tender bosom, provoking the transports of the happy priest who administers with her. She is about twenty years old, has fine black eyes and hair, is very genteel, and full of spirits.

Mifs Fra–r, No. 6, *Queen-street, Golden square.*

The ridiculous distinctions which tradesmen make among one another, were the actual means of placing Miss F– in her present situation. We may see every day a wholesale dealer look upon a retailer as infinitely below him, and even the Tallow-chandler treats the Butcher with contempt, the Butcher in his turn looks down on the poor Barber; and the Barber has his triumph over the Blacksmith and the keeper of a Chandler's shop; none put themselves on an equality with all except the Attorney, who has an opportunity of profiting by other people's weakness and absurdities. Nancy is the daughter of a Tradesman, and was taught by her parents not for the world to keep company with Miss Rappee, the Tobacconist's daughter; who, in her turn was taught to despise the Cheesemonger's family: the consequence of which was, that being taught to look so much above their own sphere, they became an easy prey to men of fashion and were soon abandoned.

Nancy has good deal of vivacity, and a pretty face, she has a very pleasing aquiline nose, has excellent teeth, and good hair, and is good natured but rather haughty, she does not much care to give her company to any body whose person is not in some measure pleasing to her, without they make it well worth her while. She has an open manner of discourse in company, which is highly agreeable, and though she expects a genteel present, she is by no means mercenary, but enjoys the sport with all the vigorous ardour that may be expected from a girl of one and twenty.

Mifs Go–ld, No. 67, *Well-ftreet*.

Every woman has not the same talents to please alike, yet, all have some peculiar to themselves; the one sings, another dances with a peculiar grace. One charms by her sense and sensibility; another catches the heart by mere simplicity. Miss Go–ld's particular advantage is a surprising fond humour which she displays in the most

agreeable manner imaginable. A mistress of such a turn, must sure be very desirable, as nothing in the world can please equal to good humour, joined with beauty. This lady lives in very gay life, and receives visits only from the best, of whom she makes whatever she thinks proper, by help of her agreeable talent. She is but slim made, is not above twenty years old, has fine dark brown glossy hair and eyes.

Mifs Ric–fon, No. 14, *Titchfield-street.*

Her heaving breast with rapture lies,
And love her every wish supplies.

The constraint put upon the Inclination of most young girls, proves very often an irresistible enticement for them to indulge them – Miss R– is an instance of this, her mother, by endeavouring to control her, raised the fire of desire in her breast, and she soon became a convert to love and libertinism – She is fond of the sport to excess, and, by her own account, has never yet been bless'd with a *satisfying meal* of *manhood*. She never consults the person of a man, for she cannot like him without he has *extraordinary powers*, which are the only *credentials* by which a person can recommend themselves to her.

She is about twenty-four, has a fair skin, and good eyes; is very full breasted, and has an agreeable lisp in her speech; she has genteel and good clothes, but dresses in a stile peculiar to herself.

Miſs Wilſ–n, No. 11, *Green-ſtreet, Cavendish-square.*

'Tis now before you, and the pow'r to chuse.

Miss W–n is about twenty-four, light hair, rather above the common size. How such a piece of goods first came to our market we are at a loss to guess; we have indeed heard that she lived for some time servant in Wapping; and, as the tars are good-natured, free-hearted fellows, and, after long voyages, are not very nice in their choice, they might perhaps have done her a good-natured action; this is the only way we can account for it, every other seems absurd to us. Her hands and arms, her limbs, indeed, in general, are more calculated for the milk-carrier, than the soft delights of love; however, if she finds herself but in small estimation with our sex, she repays them the compliment, and frequently declares that a female bed-fellow can give more real joys than ever she experienced with the male part of the sex; perhaps her demands in that way may be so great that she never found a man able to supply her; this is but a natural conclusion, when a lady is remarked for paying visits to a fellow only famous for idiotism. The proverb indeed is on her side, and perhaps she has found it true. The ingenious author of the *Woman of Pleasure* has given us a noble picture of it in the foolish nosegay man.

Many of the pranks she has played with her own sex in bed

(where she is as lascivious as a goat) have come to our knowledge; but, from our regard to the delicacy of the sex, are suppressed, but in no sort as a favour to her; our plan indeed is too confined to admit of it: but we can assure her, unless she gives over that scandalous itch of hers, to sow dissentions where harmony and peace should ever reign, and which she envies because she cannot attain to – we shall not forget her next year, but be more explicit – and moreover acquaint her drone of a keeper.

Mrs. Chif–lme, No. 11, *Berner-ſtreet*.

Gallants beware, look sharp, take care,
The blind cat many a fly.

This lady whose genteel behaviour, animated with no small degree of vanity, might persuade one, from her first appearance, that she is a modest woman, is, nevertheless, among the number of come-at-able demireps, who meet you in a *tete-a-tete*, about three quarters of the way, to prevent mistakes from external prudery. She is, it must be acknowledged, a pretty little woman, has good eyes and fine hair, a handsome hand and arm, and a great deal of that small talk which women of this cast are so apt to take for pleasantry and wit. Her apparent disinterestedness is very seducing, as she puts on all the airs of a woman of consequence, whose sole vice in an intrigue is pleasure; but beneath this delusion, self-interest may easily be discriminated. She is, indeed, at the time of life when prudence ought to predominate over every passion; and yet women of about four and thirty lose sight of it the most, and require the greatest indulgence. Philosophers account for it if you can! I will, in the mean while, hazard a conjecture from experience. When a woman perceives her charms decay, and finds every day estranges her still farther from her juvenile beauty, she regrets (if an amorous woman) the loss of every moment of her life that has not been consecrated to bliss, and risks an adventure that she would formerly have spurned, rather than lose the chance of an admirer, the perspective of a moment's enjoyment; by her late appearance, we suppose her much reduced.

This lady at present occupies the first floor, but how long she will keep it we cannot answer.

Miſs Sto–s, No. 15, *Steven-ſtreet.*

Her eyes enflam'd and sparkling too;
Her cheek, the rose and lilly's hue;
Her nose was strait, and just its height,
Her lips than coral far more bright;
Her breasts two little hills of snow;
In which two vivid rubies glow:
Tho' one might span her slender waist,
Her thighs would scarcely be embrac'd,
Her taper leg by far excell'd
All that was ever yet beheld.

What our warm poet here imagined, is in Miss St—es realized; for her face has the health of Hebe. She seems designed as the handmaid of love, and the servant of pleasure.

Her eyes sparkle, and emanate the flames which seem to glow in her bosom; and inspire that life, fire, and vivacity which animates her conversation.

Her make is as elegant as imagination can paint. She is a very agreeable companion, and remarkable for her generosity; so that she is an object well worthy of the pursuit of a *man of pleasure*; yet in that pursuit, if he wishes the true pleasure resulting from the society of a desirable woman, he must prevent her drinking too much. She is about nineteen, and expects a brace of shiners.

Miſs Molesw–h, No. 22, *Oxendon-ſtreet*.

Her youthful blood is all on fire,
She is all love and hot desire;
Her pulse beats high, her bosom heaves,
The more is done the more she craves.

The novelty of this nymph upon town, must give her high recommendation to those who *letch* is a *new face*. She has however, other strong recommendations in the art she has adopted; for, besides being a very well made girl, with a very agreeable countenance, she is perfectly *mistress of attitudes*, and knows all the workings of *human nature*. Yet she is very decent and modest in company; and, though perfectly conversant in all that small talk which makes woman appear well educated, and is therefore very chatty, yet never known to swear. From being unhackneyed in her business, she is incapable of drinking; and we, for that, as well as other mysterious reasons, think her a very desirable companion, of only about nineteen years of age.

If you should think it necessary to enquire her perfections further apply as above, and, on a proper recommendation, marked in gold 'George the Third,' she will herself, give you a more full and better satisfaction as to her abilities *in bed*.

Miſs Br–ley, No. 61, *South Moulton-street*.

The principal attractions of a female, in a public line of life are not to be confined merely to person. We have had frequent occasion to observe this in our review, but happy it is for those who wanting such attractions, can substitute others in lieu of them.

This lady has had that good fortune, and her agreeableness stands in lieu of *beauty*; for her face is in lack of such perfection, she has, however, a very good eye, which would alone be no small recommendation. But what recommends her much more, is a pleasantry which makes her courted as the *laughter-loving* goddess, and the patroness of mirth and good-humour, every where; this, in no small degree is assisted by a very good education, and good temper, which alike prevent her from swearing and drinking: and, in the whole, render her an object of esteem and attention. She is about twenty years of age, and ever satisfied with a single guinea.

This lady is said to be the natural daughter of L–d B–, and is of a fair complexion.

Mifs Lef–r, No. 23, *Upper Newman-street.*

Under how hard a fate are women born;
Prais'd to their ruin, or exposed to scorn!
If they want beauty, they of love despair,
And are besieg'd like frontier towns if fair.

This lady was a few years since, a servant in a gentleman's family, near Holborn: in which capacity she used frequently to walk for the air, with her little ward, in Gray's Inn Gardens. A certain gentleman of the law, perceiving a very fine girl, which she was at that time, often in the walks, took the opportunity of conversing with her, and soon after persuaded her to come and make some tea for him in his chambers. The sequel, it were needless to relate: she was debauched, and soon after deserted by her betrayer. The consequence of which was, having lost her place, and being destitute of a character, she was obliged to have recourse to her beauty for a subsistence. She took lodgings near Red Lyon Square, and had a number of successive admirers. She was, at this time, not above twenty; tall and well made, with a fine open expressive countenance, large amorous eyes; her other features in due symmetry; her mouth very agreeable, and her teeth regular; in a word, she was at that time one of the finest women upon the town, and, accordingly, made one of the best figures from the emoluments of her employments. She was some time after taken into keeping by a man of fortune, with whom she made a summer excursion into the country; but, upon his demise, her finances being exhausted, she was compelled to have recourse to a more general commerce, in which she has not been so successful, as before; and chagrin added to the usual irregularities accidental to her profession, has diminished those charms which were before so attracting; her face is now rather bloated, and she is grown somewhat masculine in her person; she may, nevertheless, still be pronounced a very good piece, and a desirable woman.

Mifs Towns–d, No. 12, *Gress-street.*

The God of love with all his darts,
Lives in her eyes to conquer hearts.

This lady adds to a genteel person, an excellent understanding; having had good success, she has been prudent enough to be saving, so as to enable herself to appear in an elegant manner, and to be provided in cafe of an emergency.

She is visited by liberal company, for no others are welcome to her as mere visitors. She is about twenty, has a fair face, with delicate and well formed features, her forehead is beautifully spacious, and she has a very handsome mouth, with good teeth, and is an almost constant attendant at the places of amusement, where she is well known by the men of pleasure, and is held in estimation by them, being universally allowed to be a very desirable woman.

———————————

Miſs Char–ton, same house as the last lady.

Heaven in her eye,
In every motion ectacy and love.

This is an old observation, but certainly a true one, that some of the finest women in England are those, who go under the denomination of ladies of easy virtue. Miss C– is a particular instance of the assertion; she came of reputable parents, bred delicately, and her education far superior to the vulgar; yet the address of a designing villain, too soon found means to ruin her; forsaken by her friends, pursued by shame and necessity; she had no other alternative, than to turn –, let the reader guess what. – She was long a favourite among the great, but some misconduct of hers, not to be accounted for, reduced to the servile and detestable state of turning common. She is a fine figure, tall and genteel, has a fair round face, with a faint tinge of that bloom she once possessed, is rather melancholy, 'till inspired with a glass, and then is very entertaining company.

She lodges on the first floor, however, with the assistance of the last lady, who lives in the parlour, they sport a chariot, but some times the wheels get off, owing, we suppose, to the cash being low.

Mifs Will–s, No. 6, *Princess-street, Cavendish-square.*

Temptation strong, who can withstand?
When push'd to it hard with sword in hand.

A few years ago, at the time when that celebrated fair, called Bartholomew Fair was held, Miss W– went with some young women to see the diversions of that place, there were a parcel of young bucks singled her out immediately, one of them stuck to close to her, took her round the fair, and bought her several trinkets; at last he prevailed on her to drop her acquaintances, as he did his, and to go in to the crown to dance; he kept her there till towards morning, and then had not much difficulty, (being warm with wine and dancing) to persuade her to go to his bed; next day being afraid to go home again, she consented to lie with him, which she did for some time, and then parted by mutual consent; since that time she has lived on the town, and in different parts of it; dresses extremely genteel, is tall and lusty, has brown hair, black eyes, fair skin, and fresh colour, is rather delicate in her choice of customers , and high in her demands.

Mrs. Ha–on, No. 4, *York-street, Queen Ann Street*.

Be cautious, ye fair, of the man your trust.

A good pretty Scotch lass of about twenty-four, strong features, dark hair, and eyes, with extraordinary good teeth, She was debauched by a Scotch gentleman in the army; but finding an opportunity to marry, he left her with a small present; promising her great things when he came into his wife's fortune, which was said to be considerable; but as this proved only a pretence to get rid of her, she was obliged to shift for herself and make the most of her person: she has some extraordinary good acquaintance, and does as well as most of her sisterhood.

She is always to be seen at the parlour window; her price is one pound one, but, like many others of the fraternity, will not turn her back on a less sum, she will rather accept of half a guinea, than her friend should return home with his burthen.

Miſs Gronmoſ–d, No. 59, *South Moulton-street.*

O! Parents, consider the child in future.

This is a decent, well-bred, young lady, about twenty-two, was brought up in France, her father being a man who had an extreme good place for life, during which period he could very well afford to bring her up in the way he did; but being too ambitious was the cause of her ruin; after his decease she was left to the wide world to shift for herself, her mother dying when she was very young. Which way to turn herself she knew not: the whole of her father's effects went to pay some debts, so that being totally out of subsistence, she applied to one of those handy old women who oblige gentlemen with the newest ware, an opportunity which to her seemed the *dernier* resource, consequently was resolved to embrace it: in short, after loosing her maidenhood for a trifling consideration, she was obliged to commence trader, and has for some time past obtained a decent livelihood.

She is a very elegant, genteel fair girl, light hair, and extremely fine skin; her price is from two to five guineas.

Mrs. Harris–n, next door to the Shoemaker's Shop, *Cleveland-ſtreet, New Moulton-ſtreet.*

Let the present hour be mine.

A pompous heroic girl, without either wit or humour, but fancies herself clever without any person acquiescing with her whomsoever. She is of the red-haired kind and very vicious, too fond of the male kind for her business, which is the cause of her not succeeding as she should do. Her person is extremely well made, good eyes, fair skin, and incomparable fine hair; never so happy as when in bed with a pretty fellow, altho' she gets nothing by him – like the giddy girl, thinks of nothing but the present, leaving all future events to chance. She left an elderly man, who would have given her five guineas, to bed with a young fellow who had not a single sixpence, and having herself just one guinea thought it sufficient to defray the expense of the night and the following day, leaving herself without a farthing for the sake of a few hours indulgence with this favourite. Whatever money she receives from her indifferent customers, she holds in a kind of contempt, and longs for an opportunity to throw it away upon her favourite man – generally one who is penniless and glad of even a dinner.

This lady lives in the first floor, was lately in keeping with a young banker, but is since with another gentleman.

Mifs Sh–rd, No. 46, *Goodge-street.*

A woman if she's young and fair,
Of lovers never need despair.

A very desirable companion, though in the *knowing* stile she is *up* to *a thing or two*, and is not to be had by a *queer cull*. She is of a middle size, inclined to be fat, and may be said, if we draw a *kind view* of things, or argued *o posteriori*, to incline to the *luscious*.

Her face is one of those where love seems to have chosen his seat for casting his darts from, especially from her eyes, which, from a certain peculiar cast, is all life, spirit, and fire; indeed, it seems rather to flame than burn. Her hand and arm are uncommonly neat; and her leg, thigh, and the *demesnes* adjacent remarkably tempting.

She drinks but a little, swears less, and has that great attractive recommendation to every woman – an apparent modesty, which, if a woman wants the reality is certainly the best substitute for it. She is without doubt a most pleasing *pupil* of *pleasure*, and perfectly competent to the instruction of those who desire to be announced *Students* in the *mysteries of Venus*. She is about 20, and a single guinea will content her.

This lady's apartments are on the first floor; has several city friends, and lawyers from Gray's Inn and the Temple.

Miſs Mo–e, No. 1, *Charles-street, Newman-street.*

Such is the power of good nature, that it can stand in the place of the other requisites usually expected to be found in the followers of the mysteries of Venus. Beauty, which is *arcanum*, tho' the cosmetics which adulterate it are, the first and chief requisite; and next to it, an agreeable conversation. Here, however, is the reverse of the medal! For Miss M–e, has nothing to boast of in point of beauty, as she has but a middling face, with large features, a coarse hand and arm, and in stature short and clumsy. So much for her person. Next, as to her conversation, she is ignorance itself; yet good nature has force enough to bewitch and to continue the spell over those whom it has once bound.

Her age is about nineteen, and her favours may be had on very moderate terms.

She is an excellent bedfellow, being fond of the sport, and is just from the country.

Mrs. Abbing–on, next door to the Butcher's shop, *Store-street*.

In vain for youth we all contend,
Age to beauty will soon put an end.

This lady was born of a good family, but being naturally of a forward disposition, she found means to deceive her parents, when a young Hibernian, who seeking out the natural bent of her inclinations, soon found an easy access to the fortress he had long been waiting to storm; but her father dying soon afterwards, my young gentleman was disappointed in his hopes of possessing any fortune at his decease, and therefore soon gave her an opportunity to seek for another keeper, which was one Mr. A–, whose name she now assumes. She lived with him as his wife for some time; he dying, she was again left to shift for herself; but, with prudence and industry, she soon acquired money sufficient to furnish a house.

She is genteel, dark hair, black eyes, neat ankles, and about the middle size, is about the age of forty, though seldom own herself above twenty-five, remarkable for her amorous disposition, and earnest desire to please her customers, whom she would rather treat in her turn, than part without being both mutually satisfied.

Mrs. Cor–ish, No. 66, *Well-street.*

A wanton widow, of a middle size, black eyes, plump made, and her skin good.

She is commonly at home at her apartments, which are very genteel, neat and elegant. Has a good set of friends, therefore is seldom seen at any public place of resort without an acquaintance.

Her behaviour is very genteel when she has mind, but can upon an occasion let fly a volley of small shot; but who, when they are provoked, have an absolute command of their tongue? Her dress is always in taste, and indeed rather elegant than otherwise.

She has always five or six ladies of her own stamp in the house with her; so is able to suit any gentleman with a young tit bit, and by that means she has a very comfortable livelihood.

———————————————

Mrs. Will–ms, No. 17, *Pit-ſtreet.*

Fond she is and e'er will be.
Of our king's new guineas.

This is a fine tall lady, about twenty-four, a very fine figure, just returned from Brighton, has been in dock to have her bottom cleaned and fresh coppered, where she has washed away all the impurities of prostitution, and risen almost immaculate, like Venus, from the waves. She is now fit to carry any burthen, and sails from the rate of ten to twelve *notches* an hour. If the spring and even the summer of her beauty be past, she is not without hopes of a fruitful autumn. She at present has a young man of the pen who is her favourite, and lives on the first floor. Her footing is rather superior to the common run, and expects five pieces, but being often disappointed, is very well pleased with two or three.

Mrs. Elli–t, No. 24, *Pit-street.*

If in search of game you rove,
For to sooth your melancholy:
Here you may give a loose to love,
With one that's lovely, brisk and jolly,

Mrs. E–t is the only child of an eminent tradesman in London, who brought her up, and educated her in the best manner, but being fond of dress, even to an extreme, her father could not satisfy her in all her desires, for which reason, and through the persuasions of a young officer who lodged in the house, she went away with him, to become a fine lady, but after he had got what he wanted, he changed his quarters; Mrs. E–t was afraid to go home again, so she went and offered herself at a Bagnio; she was accepted being a fine girl, but was soon taken from thence into keeping by an old Letcher; she did not stay long with him, but

has shifted her keepers and lodgings many times:
she now is at free liberty to trade upon her own
bottom: is tall and comely, fair skin, light hair,
blue eyes, and lively disposition; price high.

Mifs Jo–es, No. 16, *Edward-street, Cavendish-square.*

Thro' various scenes of untir'd, Miss J–es
     has run
And still to please she does, the best she can:
Her well taught limbs, will twist, and turn,
     and wind,
What more can wanton do; to suit your mind.

This lady was born in the country, but the
circumstances of her parents, when she was
sufficiently grown up, obliged them to send
her into London to get a livelihood, she was
not long before she got a place in St. James's
Market, where, whither, by being accustomed
to see the poor lambs bleed, or rather a desire
of becoming a sacrifice to the goddess of love, is

left for the reader to judge, but she was shortly
found stabbed to the heart in the most tender
and susceptible part of her body, in short she
was unable to withstand the powerful impulse
of nature any longer, so was ravished with her
own consent, at the age of sixteen; her mistress
on the discovery, thought proper to send her
going, for fear her good man should take it in
his head to kill the lamb over again. She began
now to show the bent of her inclinations, she
listed under the banners of Cupid, and marched
at the head, being of a courageous disposition,
and always ready to obey standing orders;
she had great success, and often made the
enemy to yield, by which means she gained no
inconsiderable share of spoil, but her charitable
disposition, (being always ready to relieve the
naked and needy) soon reduced her. Her places
of residence have been various; she is now
about twenty-six, and though she has been
many times besieged, and innumerable times
bombarded; she looks well, and is remarkable
for her gentleness and affability.

Mifs Lawr–e, No. 6, *Church-street, St. Ann's, Soho.*

The religion of the Jews will not permit them to eat pork, or feast with Christians; how strictly this lady may adhere to particulars in her articles of faith we cannot positively tell; but this we can say for truth, that she has not the least objection to Christian concupiscence, and will open her synagogue of love even on the Sabbath, either to Jew, Turk, or Infidel, if they think proper to call on her as above.

This young Israelite renounced her Levitical friends for the sake of a Christian, who gave inward proofs of a new faith, which were so convincing to her that she has continued a thorough orthodox convert ever since. She is of a sprightly disposition, has good teeth, dark

hair, black eyes, a roman nose, a fresh colour, of a middle size, and is very wanton in her looks.

Miſs Wa–s, No. 60, *South Moulton-street.*

Is ever kissing, toying, shoving,
And knows no end of lust but loving.

Our nymph seems cast by nature in one of the happiest moulds and happiest hours of love. She is tall and elegantly made, with a fair complexion, and about nineteen years of age: her eyes seem to beat an alarm to that of love, which her tongue, one would suppose, would invite to a parley with. Her foot and leg have the shape which statuaries give to the Medicean Venus; and the drapery of the figure exceeds even the beauty of it; for she is always dressed elegantly, and in a stile of the first fashion.

Having said so much of the perfections of this lady, it is but just to give the remaining part of her character, rather in hopes of her amending than to condemn her, for an object, who, in the words of my motto, is *ever loving*, and is so peculiarly adapted for that business, ought to seize upon every means of increasing her charms.

Her companionableness is destroyed by her being fretful and tenacious; and her opinion of herself extends from her person to her conversation, of which she is vain though ignorant. But her principal defect is of a love of money, which she seems to prefer to every thing; for though she is fond of the sport, and admires a *master of arts*, yet she would forsake even such a one so great is her mercenary disposition, if she should have the fortune to light on a *pigeon*.

She drives a chariot, has several city friends, both bankers and Israelites.

Mifs We–ls, No. 35, *Newman-ftreet.*

Virtue is the surest guide.

This is a young genteel girl, of the Welch breed, and of which she is not a little proud, and thinks that the blood of Owen Tudor runs in her veins; she is willing to do business with any one. She is as wild as a goat, of a sandy colour, her features are small, and is a tight little piece.

This lady is said to be the daughter of a farmer in Wales, who sent her to London very young, to be under the care of an aunt, with whom the she had not long resided before a young gentleman ingratiated him so far into her graces, as to gain her consent to make him happy by her ruin, under a promise of marriage – but no sooner had enjoyment damped the ardour of his love, than he abandoned her to the reproaches and calumny of a merciless world; 'till at length with shame and disappointment she quitted her aunt's, and entered on the town.

There is one thing to be said of her, which is, if she had not quitted the paths of virtue, she might have proved an honour and an ornament to her sex, as she is possessed of every good and amiable quality to make this true.

Her customers, whenever inclined to pay her a visit, are always sure to be received with a behaviour and politeness becoming a person in a higher station.

She is like many others, mighty good humoured when pleased. If you give her a piece of gold, before you enter the premises, she goes to work with great affability and sweetness of temper; but if not, she is cool enough, and thinks of nothing but the money during the time of enjoyment.

Mifs Wats–n, No. 36, *Well-street.*

Fortune, we all know, is a precarious Goddess, for although she smiles with the most enchanting grace, it is like an April day, when the sun shines delightfully, yet is suddenly over clouded. Miss Nancy was educated with the utmost degree of parental tenderness, and taught all the polite necessaries for female education which those in expectation of fortune generally have, and hers were not small; but alas! who can dive into the mysteries of fate. Her dependence was upon an old uncle, a Batchelor, who always promised her a very handsome fortune, but that arch rogue Cupid

shot the old man, one day thro' the bright eyes
of a buxom widow; in short he married her, and
in a twelvemonth had a child by her, but dying
soon after, bequeathed his whole fortune to his
wife and child, and left poor Nancy without a
farthing. This was a terrible circumstance, as
she had long been solicited by a young citizen
in trade, of whom she was dotingly fond, but
he declined his visits when he heard of her fate;
this has such an effect on her, that it threw her
into a fit of illness, which had like to have cost
her, her life. This brought her artful swain to
visit her, and when she got a little better, he
took a country lodging for her. And in a short
time got the better of her virtue; he kept her
genteel for some time, but finding it expensive,
frankly told her he could not afford it, and so
left her. Poor Nancy was in a terrible situation,
but finding no other remedy, determined to
enlist herself in the train of Venus, where she
has continued ever since; her customers are
chiefly citizens, who visit very privately. She
lives elegant, and is a great œconomist, is tall
and genteel, about twenty-four years of age,
rather dark complexion, a little pitied with the

small pox, her price is one pound one, but will not refuse half a guinea.

She is in good condition for a journey being possessed of long legs and is a first floor lodger.

Mifs G–ge, No.13, *South Moulton-street.*

This lady has not been in business long; she surrendered her citadel to a captain of the navy, who in his attack upon her, united the seaman with the lover, and the ingenuity of the one won her heart as much as the passion of the other. As a specimen of his epistolary method of corresponding with her, we shall subjoin a part of one of his letters to her, which runs exactly thus; he tells her that he had often thought to reveal to her the tempests of his heart by word of mouth, to scale the walls of her affection, but terrified with the strength of her fortifications, he had concluded to make more regular approaches, to attack her at farther distance, and try what a bombardment of letters would do, whether those carcases of love thrown into the sconces of her eyes, would break into the midst of her breast, beat down the out-guard of her aversion and indifference, and blow up the magazine of her cruelty, that she might be brought to terms of capitulation: which indeed she soon was, and upon reasonable terms. The captain was with her but a short time, being obliged to repair to his station; and after his departure, she was kept by one in the army, who was obliged to give way to the more *powerful* solicitations of one of greater force. She is just thirty, pretty and amorous, has a charming lively eye and a handsome mouth; she is rather short but very delicately made, a charming colour which seems to be natural, is finely diffused over her cheeks, and sets her face off to great advantage, and she has fine brown hair, is good temper'd, and very free and merry.

She drives a very handsome curricle, and is in keeping by a Mr. C–ns.

Mrs. Str–ls, No.88, *Queen Ann Street Eaſt*.

Her little heart, beats raptures to the joy;
And love, from morn to night, is her
employ.

This lady keeps the house, is a fat plump lass, about twenty-four years of age, and is at present in keeping with a country parson, who is seldom in town.

Much experience, and a natural propensity to the business, has rendered this lady a perfect mistress in the science she professes; and notwithstanding her great practice, she is not the least tired of it, but pursues it with as much eagerness as at first, though her long study has somewhat impaired her complexion, which she endeavours to disguise, by the assistance of art.

The most luxurious appetite of a pampered priest might be satisfied with such a banquet as this, if there was any truth in the tales related of Jove's descending to embrace some beautiful mortal, he would certainly, before now, have had a *tete a-tete* with Mrs. S–.

At the beginning of her career in life, there was a particular severity in this lady's fate, who being naturally of a moist complexion, and being addressed by a number of suitors, she happened to make choice of a man who was by no means calculated to gratify the wishes of a longing girl; for, from a long course of debauchery, he had ruined his constitution; from this it may be reasonably supposed, that they were not long together. She soon found another to supply his deficiency. She loves a manly young bedfellow beyond every other felicity; and though she will not accept a trifle, she is by no means mercenary, for she will rather generously give a favour gratis, than accept of what she calls a dirty present.

Mrs. R–ssell, No. 17, *Fludger-street, Westminster.*

Is a fine plump girl, at the age of twenty-eight, rather dark hair and eyes, she keeps a house, and sometimes sports a chariot.

This lady has been some years in the service, in London, where she was much in vogue with the bucks and bloods of the town, who admired her more for her vulgarity than anything else, she being extremely expert at uncommon oaths, and, at her first commencing a lady of pleasure, she threw off all restraint, so that her modesty was never offended: her readiness to reveal all the secrets, which the delicate part of the sex think proper to conceal, brought her a number of clients among the youth, who are fond of beholding that mouth of the devil from whence all corruption issueth. These she took care to fleece sufficiently; so that by her economy, she is now enabled to keep her country house and receives visits from only a few, and has in some degree left off her habit of swearing.

This lady being a very good pen-woman, and much out of town, has a good opportunity of displaying her talents in that line to her lovers.

Mrs. H–rvey, No. 6 *Upper Newman-street.*

Here is a tall genteel lady, about twenty-six; as she is passionately fond of music and dancing, it may be reasonably presumed, that a small share of sport will not gratify the large desires she has for fun, and that rather than be foiled at her favourite diversion, she will set open her front door to any one who can enter in a gentleman-like and manly manner.

She has followed dancing to that degree, that it had nearly consigned her to last home; she at present is retired into the country, in hopes to gain that strength which will enable her to return to her former pleasures. Though in the country is not without a friend, for she has Mr. J– of the P– Office with her. It is supposed she will be soon in town.

This is a brown beauty, and very agreeable, has fine eyes, and a good set of teeth. She became a

proselyte to the sport of Venus very young, at
what age we cannot tell, neither can we satisfy
the reader whether she ever was married or not.
She is a firm votary to the wanton goddess, and
does not despise the good Bacchus, to whose rosy
smiling cheeks she will often toss off a sparkling
bumper. She is very active and nimble, and not
a little clever in the performance of the act of
friction, which renders her the more agreeable
to all who have the pleasure of her embraces.
We are told she always makes it a point to be
faithful to her admirers. We wish all the ladies
of her profession would act in the same manner.

She is a lady of great sensibility, not that her
feelings are painful to her, far otherwise, the
more her tender sensations are touched, the
more pleased she is, she is much delighted with
All for love, and would relinquish her share in
the government of the world for that darling
passion; she thinks herself every way qualified
to perform the part of Cleopatra, when ever she
can meet with Mark Anthony; she lives in a very
convenient house, and is pretty much visited.

She has been for some years a votary at the
temple of Venus, and it may with truth be asserted,

that she understands the up-and-down art of her posteriors as well as any lady of her profession. She has been so good a friend to the good old cause, that the number of travellers who have gone the path to the fountain of love have trodden all the grass away. This attracts a number of Votaries, whose curiosity leads them to examine those curious parts. She is open, generous, and free. She takes the utmost pains imaginable to improve her acquaintance with the best, by going every day to some of the most eminent shops when in town, where she generally makes acquaintance with some young fool of quality or other, who supports her in her extravagance to the utmost pitch of vanity.

She has always been remarkably happy in her connexions; among her other attractions when the sport is over, you may listen to the melody of her voice until nature again revives, which she will endeavour, by all the art she is mistress of, shall not be long first.

Miſs Co–way, No. 50, *Slone-ſquare.*

Hail beauty, such is thine electric touch,
It fills the veins, and animates the pulse
Of all who but behold thee!

If we were called upon to name the lady whom we conceive to be handsome, it would certainly be the one we are now speaking of; she has so many enchanting graces, that they are quite irresistible. It is impossible to withstand the artillery of her eyes, as the winged lightening; then her hair, her lips, her every thing, are so transporting charming as to fill every beholder with rapture.

She is just twenty-two, of a most elegant form, and as we know her to be amorously inclined, we do not think that any young fellow need despair, if he has ability, and understands the method of bringing a thing to an end.

This lady has been several years in trade, and never in want of business. She was lately in keeping by L– S–, who was fond of her to excess. She was early initiated in the science of love, and she is determined to loose no time, while youth and vigour will give her leave to love; on any other subject, she is a woman of the strictest honour and generosity, has a free and open heart, is very agreeable, and her admirers never find that either their money or time is thrown away.

Her education has been liberal; her conversation is easy and unaffected; her taste for literature would not disgrace the greatest genius of the age, and if we could pass over in silence her present mode of life, she has every qualification that would render her an ornament to the female world.

This lady lives in very high life, is not in keeping now, tho' she has had many very genteel overtures made to her on that account; variety is her delight, and she indulges her inclination to the utmost degree; yet 'tis said she has a favourite who is a foreigner and partakes of her purse as well as her favours.

She is fond of *play*, and never yet could meet her match at *all-fours*, for she *begs* one at the end of every *deal*, and seldom fails *succeeding* in her request till she has entirely beat her antagonist, who, like more losing gamesters, generally wishes to renew the *game*, when all his *cash* is *spent* and he is least able.

Miſs B–lford, *Titchfield-street.*

The British fair to manly hearts inclin'd,
Their passions open and their souls unbind,
'Tis nature prompts, what harm can be in
        this,
To give and take from each the balmy kiss.

This child of love looks very well when drest. She is rather subject to fits, alias counterfeits, very partial to a Pantomime Player at Covent Garden Theatre. She may be about nineteen, very genteel, with a beautiful neck and chest, and most elegantly moulded breasts, her eyes are wonderfully piercing and expressive. She is always lively, merry, and cheerful, and in bed, will give you such convincing proofs of her attachment to love's game, that if you leave one guinea behind, you will certainly be tempted to renew your visits.

Mrs. V–cent, *Wardour-street*.

> She'll nicely chose and neatly spread,
> Upon her cheek's the best French red.

This lady is about thirty, not of very advantageous stature, but her fine eyes cannot be looked upon without exciting all the thrilling emotions of desire in the soul of the beholder. She keeps the house, and is to be met with in the parlour, all her apartments being let-out; nothing under gold will be here accepted.

Mifs V–ghan, No. 24, *Upper Newman-street.*

Give me but thee, I will make a heav'n of
      earth,
Each night should give to new-born
      pleasures birth.
The fun of joy should paint continual noon,
And e'en on age of Noah pass on too soon.

This priestess of Venus is of a dark complexion,
dark hair, and expressive eyes of the same
colour. She is about twenty-one, rather a
pretty genteel girl; she seems to be a pupil
of Cato, whose opinion it was that a woman
should divest herself of her modesty with
her clothes. The scandalous chronicle says,
she had a child by a coachman about nine
months ago, whether it be true or not, she
is nevertheless as agreeable a companion in
bed, as she is a pleasing one out of it. She is
tolerably reasonable, being very well satisfied
with a guinea per night.

———————————————

Mrs. D–nby, No. 82, *Queen Ann-street.*

A bird in the hand is worth two in the bush,
Or never let the Goldfinches hop the twig.

A fine plump lady, twenty-four years old, rather
short, with sandy colour hair, fine blue eyes,
rather of an amorous constitution; when in the
arms of an equally lewd partner, she never wishes
to fall in the arms of sleep, whilst Venus holds
her court, Morpheus is kicked out of doors, as
she keeps the house, any gentleman may have a
night's lodging for one pound one shilling, and
half the money, if he can do the business well.

Mrs. B–ooks, next to the Pawnbroker, *Newman-street.*

Nature is nature Lalirus.
Let the wife say what she will.

A genteel lady, about twenty-three, very keen,
as you may judge by her eyes, as she looks both

ways at once, however she is tolerable well made, with well formed projecting bubbies, that defy the result of any manual pressure, panting and glowing with unfeigned desire, and soon inviting the gratification of senses. As she keeps the house, any gentleman may with something less than a bank note, be admitted into her *Sanctum Sanctorum*.

Mifs P–ctor, *Cursitor-ftreet, formerly of Gress-street*.

I am the lass whose ever open arms,
Both day and night stand ready to receive,
The fierce assaults of Briton's amorous sons.

A nice girl about nineteen, lives in the first floor, her motive for moving was solely on account of some Temple friends, namely Attorneys, Counsellors, and Clerks in office. She never rises before twelve, after which time she may be seen, ready to undress and go again to bed. She frequents the Theatre where she gets an innumerable acquaintance; as a chatty, agreeable companion, her company must be courted by those who love a dish of *chit chat* to be served up first. She dresses well, but rather flighty; she is seldom tired of love's game, whilst the *blind boy* can find the way *in*, and is able to pay the *toll*, before he comes *out*; very cunning and never returns money after the curtain is drawn up. Price one pound one.

———————————

Miſs W–by, No. 3, *Gress-street. Rathbone-place.*

—— So beauteous young and gay,
And dearly loves the am'ruos play.

A pleasing countenance, of a middling size, her features are the delicacy of a court lady in their *town use*. This pretty little girl is about eighteen, lives in the parlour, is always to be seen in the day time, as she never dresses till time for the Theatres; in bed she performs all her paces in a pleasing manner, and keeps exact time to every motion, urges with every possible insinuations the *coming* pleasure, and returns the ecstatic with a flood of tepid delight, always urging repetitions. Her price is from half a guinea to what you please, but for a night's lodging, notice must previously be given her.

Miſs M–tague, *Meard-street.*

Where there's no path, no track, he runs
      astray,
But in a beaten road can ever find the way.

A well shaped girl about twenty-three, somewhat averse to contradiction, must have her own way; she is however, good-natured, and is said to be thoroughly experienced in the whole art and mystery of *Venus's* tactics, and can as soon reduce a perpendicular to less than the curve of a parabola; her eyes sparkle, and emanate the flames which seem to glow in her bosom, and inspire that life, fire, and vivacity which animates her conversation; she is rather generous, and you may sometimes find your way *in* there free of expense.

Miſs H–rington, *Newman-street.*

She spins her *webb* to catch male flies,
Like sportsmen's black birds – by her eyes.

A knowing one, lives in the first floor, has two or three gentlemen favourites; by giving a double rap, this lady will instantly make her appearance, and if she returns you a favourable glance, she will immediately conduct you in a very complaisant manner to a convenient sofa, and suffer you there to take a view of her *haven of delight*, where pretty ringlets hang in tempting curls over the *cupidinous font*, in return she likewise expects a view of *nature's gifts* from you, which if she thinks clean and properly adopted, she will *unload* for two pounds two. She is rather a good figure,

and about twenty-five, with a tolerable good complexion, in company chatty, witty and agreeable.

Mrs. St–ton, at the Shoe-maker's, *Corner of Upper Newman-street.*

All I ask of mortal man,
Is to – me whilst I can.

A fine plump widow bewitched, as she says, she is the wife of a captain S–n, who is gone abroad; but her passions are not to be confined, and thinking life not worth her care, without the thorough gratification of that most noble sense, she gives an uncontrolled loose to all her desires, and places the *tree of life* into the *garden of Eden*, as often as inclination invites, and opportunity gives leave; and so exquisitely toned are the most sensible parts, that all the senses seem swallowed up at once in the *gulph of Venus*; she is good-natured, and does not seem to make money so much the object of love, if she thinks she has a *flash-man* who is a *posture-master;* but is not to be had by a queer-cull. She will not refuse a guinea from any man, and will take half sooner than go without. This jolly agreeable piece lives in the first floor.

Mifs Le–, *Berwick-ftreet, Soho.*

Oh pray mamma! let me down!
You will find me the best boy in town;
I'll never while I live offend,
I promise you, you will find me mend!

This young lady is tall and genteel, and about seventeen, with sandy coloured hair, and fine blue eyes that are delicious; her complexion is delicate and fair, but we cannot refrain saying, she has a piece of the termagant about her, which, however, she qualifies with a whimsicality of humour that renders it supportable. She was debauched by a young counsellor, from a boarding-school near town, where she was apprentice. Her mistress surprising her one day with a certain *naughty* book, took her into the whipping-room, where having tied her on a horse that is always there for the use of correction, she whipped her with a large rod, made of green birch, till through fatigue, the rod dropped from her hands; the counsellor meeting with her a few days after, she told him how she had been used by her governess for the book he had lent her; he took immediately a room for her, and visited her till he went to Ireland. She found herself for some time very much embarrassed, till meeting with a merchant of the city, who is fond of the rod, she soon appeared again at the theatres, which she frequents very much.

She dresses always very elegantly, and in the season she is seldom without a most enormous nosegay of luscious flowers, which she generally wears very high on the left side of her bosom, having discovered that many gentlemen have a great partiality for that effeminate ornament. She is constantly visited by *amateurs* of birch discipline, being always furnished with brooms of green birch and of the best quality, and is always very happy to see any friend that feels himself inclinable to spend three or four guineas in her company.

Mrs. G–frey, No. 6, *Newman-street*.

Here may the brisk, and able pour,
An ocean of their liquid store.

This lady may be about thirty, rather plump, she has however, every requisite to make an agreeable bed-fellow, every nerve during the preludes to enjoyment, seem trembling alive to all the refined sensations, and every part about the frame is blessed with that corresponding aptness that cannot fail of producing the most desirable effects, neither has the too frequent use of the most bewitching spot rendered it the least callous to the joys of love; she still feels all that torrent of rapture, the mutual dissolution of two souls in liquid bliss can possible afford; meets the coming moment with uncommon ecstasy, and asks the speedy return. She is very fond of black, as she pretends to be a widow; her price is one pound one tho' ten shillings and sixpence will do.

Miſs J—nſon, No. 17, *Willow-walk, near the Dog and Duck.*

Beauty soon grows familiar to the lover,
Fades in the eye, and falls upon the sense.

This pretty filly is of a middling size near twenty, Norfolk gave her birth, her countenance is rather pleasing, with fine black eyes that are very attractive, good teeth, a fine skin, and of so amorous constitution, that in the arms of an equally lewd partner, she never wishes to fall in the arms of sleep; the *dairy hills* of delight are beautifully prominent, firm and elastic, the *sable coloured grot* below with its coral lipped *janitor* is just adopted to the sons of Venus, it is a pity this girl did not receive some sort of education, however, as there are people who admire a vulgarity of expression and a coarseness of manner which they account a kind of rustic *naiveté*, and which they prefer to the polish education or the attractions of *bieuseance*, it is no wonder if she has a few customers, tho' her clothes are always at the pawnbrokers. She seems always low spirited, except when the liquor exhilarates her spirits; extremely illiterate, ungrateful to her benefactors, peevish, addicted to swearing and to low company; this girl in a short time will be in the lowest class of prostitutes; however as she is young, she is still worthy the attention of an *amateur* who would rescue her from prostitution, as we think she still possesses a little sensibility; she is the only girl that frequents is D. and D. worth mentioning; her price from five shillings to half a guinea.

Mrs. C–ild No. 24, *Newman-street.*

Let puny foplings talk of puny bliss,
Give me luxuriant bits that courts a kiss.

This lady is of middle size, twenty-three years old, plump and fair, very wanton, wicked, blue eyes, her teeth tolerably good, her complexion of a delicate white, which, by the assistance of rouge, has the rose blended with the lilly in a very voluptuous manner: a night's swim in this ocean of delight cannot be refused by the lovers of cheerfulness and good humour, when they know it is procurable at a trifling expense, but then it must be when a particular friend with whom she lives is not expected to give any interruption, this lady keeps the house.

Mrs. M–chall, No. 52, *Margate-street.*

> Freedom in love is what I crave
> And give me this, ye mighty gods.

A fine tall elegant woman rather lusty, full eyes, she has the character of a spirited, spitefully fond bed-fellow, that will keep her spark to the *mark* of business as long as he has strength to follow his labour with any pleasure or ability, her manners are easy and polite; nor is her appearance what would class he among *rep* or *demireps*; dresses very elegantly, generally appearing with a profusion of feathers on her head dress, and a large bouquet in her bosom. This lady is now kept by a gentleman, but as he is often out of town I make no doubt that she may be spoke with.

Miſs B–df–d, No. 44, *Mortimer-ſtreet, Cavendish-square.*

If mutual love, if mutual fire,
Can add a relish to desire,
Come, ye voluptuous, to this seat;
Her willing limbs will ne'er retreat,
But cling with fervour to the kiss,
Till all the soul dissolves in bliss.

In delineating the beauties of this charming little girl, the abilities of the first literary talents should be furnished for the immediate purpose of displaying her perfections to the best advantage. This wanton and enchanting nymph is a frequent visitor of the theatres; she is particularly attached to the Haymarket, for reasons best known to herself. She dresses with considerable taste, blended with a degree of neatness the frail fair are seldom accustomed to exhibit. Her accomplishments are various and brilliant; her polite and sensible conversation reflects much credit on her education, which is said to be liberal in the extreme. – This languishing fair one, when in bed with a gentleman of her own loving disposition, is amorous to distraction – her feelings at the *critical* moment are so excessive tender that she generally occasions her *blind* visitor to *shed tears* ere he quits her *covered* apartment. Her panting orbs, pouting lips, delicate shape, love-sparkling eyes (which are dark), regular set of teeth, together with a tempting leg and foot, compose the principal attractions of this goddess of pleasure. A cheerful glass of wine is not ill bestowed on this matchless heroine.

Generosity she rewards,
Meanness she despises.

Good nature may with singular propriety be deemed a striking feature in this darling little girl. This offspring of delight is indebted to eighteen summers for the attainment of such charms as the reader may for a compliment of *five guineas* be in *full possession of.*

Mifs L–w–s, No. 36, *Wells-street, Oxford-street.*

By that smile that decks thy face,
By that dimple on thy chin,
By each loving sweet embrace,
Let me *once more enter in.*

The prolific soil of Salisbury is reported to have given *birth to this whimsical* Cyprian Goddess, a more beautiful face we never witnessed, and to her praise be it spoken, she is *not* under the smallest obligation to any *performer,*

No artificial tint adorns her lovely cheeks.

Pure nature and rosy health are her inseparable companions; her conversation displays so much *artless* simplicity, that we are positive any gentleman would conceive himself happy in having an opportunity of *standing* before this lady with a view to obtain her *mark* of *pleasure*. She has lately been in keeping with a *Ri–er*, but we greatly fear he proved himself a *bad horseman*, as the lady will not, at this time, suffer him to *enter her premises*. Pecuniary embarrassments are the reasons assigned for his being deprived her *present favours*; her visitors must not be surprised if they are addressed with expressions of a *simple* nature from this votary of wantonness. She is very expert in *milking a cow*; we mention this *acquisition* merely for the accommodation of any *gentleman* who is fond of witnessing such *sport*; her panting delicate white breasts are tempting, firm, and elastic; twelve months are scarcely elapsed since her *virgin rose* was plucked. An artist of some celebrity is said to be the fortunate seducer of her *maiden treasure*; her disposition is extremely lively; she is blessed with a pair of the most enchanting black eyes we ever beheld. It is impossible to gaze at this fascinating female without being captivated with her delightful charms; she exhibits a neat leg and foot; good-

nature is a valuable ornament to this lady.
Nineteen years is her real age, and *two pounds*
two shillings will not be rejected as a reward for
the disposal of her *favours*.

Mifs H–nd–s, No. 6, *Church-street Soho*.

Beauty like mine would warm a hermit's
       heart,
Remove his calmness and disturb his rest,
Expel religion from his sacred grove,
And all his passions soften into love.

It gives peculiar pleasure to the writer of this
biography to present the public
with as delightful a female as
ever graced the cyprian
train; if unaffected beauty
blended with extreme
good-nature   be
entitled to notice, this
charming goddess of

health must certainly attract admiration. A captain in the marines which lately with this *dying* nymph (by which name she now attunes) this lady's conversation breaths so much of the accomplished woman of fashion, that we advise none but what are *real* gentlemen to approach that shrine of this delicate fair one; her disposition is lively, amorous and engaging; her temper indisputably (*for sweetness*) surpasses any we ever have had occasion to mention; her beautiful person is not only to be seen but to be admired.

> Here you may gaze with rapture on a world of charms.

She has a wonderful art in *raising* up those of her *male friends* who are inclined to *droop* while in her enchanting company. She never wishes any gentleman to *come* a second time unless he proves himself to be a man of honour at the *first* visit; *five pounds five shillings* is the present this lady expects for the distribution of her *private concerns*. Twenty years have been devoted in bringing to perfection this adorable siren.

Miſs W–l–n, No. 27, *Litchfield-street, Soho.*

Her careless air, her easy mien and dress,
Nor art, nor perfect negligence confess:
Admir'd by all, she treads the cyprian stage,
And one and twenty is the lady's age.

The Island of Jamaica is the native soil of this
wanton cyprian female, though she cannot
boast a complexion delicately fair, yet it must
be acknowledged her features are very pleasing,
she has a brilliant tell-tale love sparkling eye,
which commonly attract admiration from most
of her *male* visitors; she is a girl of considerable
taste and fashion; *Covent Garden Theatre* is her
constant evening lounge, at which place she is
known by many of the gentlemen actors, one
of which in the vocal line is said to have been
closely connected with her; a beautiful leg and
foot adorns her charming shape, a delicate pair
of white silk stockings she likewise sports, this
addition to her dress is considered by many of
her admirers as a valuable acquisition to her
appearance; report says she dances well, her

vocal abilities are of no inconsiderable promise, as she warbles with much sweetness and science; she is pronounced an amorous bed-fellow, being spitefully loving, her conversation denotes her to be a girl of good sense, an elegant set of teeth (which for whiteness stands unrivalled in the whole cyprian corps) and dark brown tresses which flow in careless ringlets across a pair of tempting rising promontories, compose the remainder of attraction in this enchanting goddess of whim; this lady's purse discovers so much elasticity that it will contain the largest *thing* any gentleman can present her with, however not the smallest *thing* will be accepted unless accompanied with *two golden balls*; twenty-one years she is indebted for the variety of accomplishments she possesses.

Mifs L–the, No. 12, *Castle-street.* *Oxford-market.*

She wants no art to give her greater charms,
And sure 'tis heaven to die in her arms.

This lovely fountain of transport is nineteen years old, her stature tall, but quite genteel, her eyes are of a beautiful sloe black, and beam a torrent of delight at every potent glance; a sweet breath and good teeth; her breasts are in the fullest proportion and will rebound with the more grateful ardour to the hand's soft pressure; her yielding limbs, though beautiful when together, are still more ravishing when separated, her temper is affable and complaisant; an air of gaiety and tenderness breath round her, unfortunately for this girl, she has received no education, she possesses none of those happy talents which improve and heighten so much amorous delights; her face however good, is destitute of expression, her manner rather vulgar, which mark out a low original. Half a guinea is the price of admission for any of our readers to *enter* such *premises* as will not cause a moment's regret.

Mrs. D–l–v–t, No. 46, *Hanover-ſtreet, Hanover-square.*

To look at her majestic figure,
Would make you caper with more vigour!
The lightning flashing from each eye,
Would lift your soul to ecstacy!
Her bubbies o-er their boundry broke,
Quick palpitating at each stroke!
With vigor o-er the bouncing bum,
She'd tell ungovern'd boys who ruled at
       home!

This lady is about thirty, she was bred a milliner, and married very young an attorney's clerk, but as his income was not sufficient to support her in the manner she wished to live, she listened to the addresses of an American gentleman who made her a handsome allowance whilst he remained in England, and took some pains to persuade her to accompany him in his present visit to that quarter of the world, but she preferred old to new England. She is at present a housekeeper, but soon intends to quit her situation and retire to a snug lodging, as she has experimentally found that the frail sisterhood are very bad pay mistresses for first and second floors. Though not young, her charms have received no diminution from the hand of time, as she has always been very careful of herself, and eluding as much as possible the main action; she is celebrated for bush-fighting with a birchen rod, which she wields with dexterity to the uncommon gratification of many gentlemen who have occasion for this operation to rouse the Venus lurking in their veins; it is said she is very fond, as many ladies are, of handling this instrument of pain and delight; she keeps always in the house a number of excellent birch brooms and cutting rods ready made for present service; her price is various, in the birchen operation, she will not take less than half a guinea, but for the completion of bliss she never condescends to grant her favours for less than a guinea.

Mifs S–wyn, *Chelsea.*

Hail beauty, such is thine electric touch,
It fills the veins and animates the pulse,
Of all who behold thee!

This lovely female is rather tall, but elegantly
made with a most enchanting bosom, a fair
complexion and excellent features, her mouth is
small, but looks when closed like a rose when
it begins to bud, fine expressive blue eyes and
beautiful teeth; dresses most elegantly and is just
turned of sixteen, she is the natural daughter of
an Officer, who died about twelve years ago in
the East-India, and is now kept by a friend of
her father's, who had her educated at a boarding
school, and who took her from it about two years
ago; this gentleman took for her a lodging on the
King's Road, just by a lazy nursery, and like the
celebrated *Runastrokus*, is very fond of *hair combing*
preparatory to the amorous conflict; and as soon
as the hair dresser is gone, he generally begins his
operation, and comb with a tortoiseshell comb
her beautiful tresses, which are always highly
perfumed with the most odoriferous scent; when

he had done, Miss retires into her bed-room to finish her dress, then take a walk into the nursery, and soon returns to the arms of her keeper with a most beautiful bouquet in her bosom, almost as large as a broom, being passionately fond, as well as her keeper, of the sweet perfume of flowers, particularly when she celebrates the rites of Venus; and it is questionable as a certain author says, whether the enjoyment of a woman be not more luscious when dressed than in *puris naturalibus*; and it is demonstrable that one thus enjoys her in a two-fold manner, for it is an axiom in sensuality that the sight contributes very much to its gratification; by preferring her dressed, it must not be however understood to mean her when encumbered with all the articles that complete the court or ball dress: of stiff stays, she should by all means, be divested; white seems the most voluptuous dress; her hair elegantly dressed and highly perfumed; the head-dress adorned with large feathers, but an indispensable article in the dress of a young woman, is, a very large nosegay of flowers, or artificial ones well scented, and which she should wear on the left side of her bosom, as high as the ear, this mode of wearing them being reckoned exceeding lascivious, an indeed there is no appendage in the whole catalogue of female dress which raises lust so powerfully as those enormous bouquets, which our women of fashion wear, their luxurious perfume not only provoke desires, but aggravate very much venereal enjoyments; they lose, however, their effect, if not worn, as mentioned before, very high on the left side of the bosom, and monstrously large, for the larger they are, the greater their influence on the amateurs of that most effeminate ornament; but to return to our charmer, a ten pound bank note will have its due influence if properly presented, and considering the inexpressible pleasure received in the arms of this young and delicate female, we think she deserves it. She is frequently to be noticed in the green boxes of the Theatres, and in the season at Ranelagh; generally dressed in white with a profusion of feathers, and seldom without a most enormous bouquet in her bosom; she keeps a chariot, and a negro servant always attends her.

The Mifs B–yan and S–ith Sifters, No. 7, *Windmill- street, Rathbone-place.*

Miss B– is tall and thin, her complexion is dark, her sister Miss S– is plump and fair, keeps a certain musician to play her now and then some tunes; these ladies have seen their thirtieth, are still however, agreeable pieces for the winter season, to those not over nice about delicacy, both illiterate and addicted to swearing; it is said they are very dexterous at the game of the birch rod; the price of these lecherous girls varies very much, but half a guinea is always acceptable to them.

Mrs. Ho–fey, No. 30, *Crop-ftreet, Lambeth-road.*

If for the joy of love thy bosom pine,
Sweet youth approach and ease thy pain on
mine.

This young girl is about eighteen, middle size, well made, with dark eyes and chestnut hair; she is very affable and engaging in her disposition, and calls forth all her powers to give delight with uncommon success, and as she is abundantly supplied with that ornamental exuberance, we cannot without doing her a signal injustice, suspect her of an indifferent to those pleasures which no woman is more capable of communicating than she is, any gentleman, possessing a superfluous half a guinea, will find her a desirable companion.

Miſs –, at Mrs. Ross's, No. 7, *Wardour-street*.

Sure heav'n alone such graces can bestow,
Where Nature's richest tints superbly glow;
What pencil can do justice to the fair;
So regular her form, so sweet her air,
Each glance the coldest, densest, breast must
      move
To taste with her the richest joys of love.

Novelty, which in the lover's calendar, is always marked with a red letter, must excite the curious to experience its charms with this dear girl; she seems indeed to have collected a considerable share of the lightning to frequent in mountainous places, and darts such irresistible glances as can scarcely fail to engage the hearts of the beholders. The barren unfrequented paths of Wales she thought too confined a situation to exert her power in, and has therefore transferred her empire to the great mart for beauty, where merit, such as hers, surely cannot fail of the most brilliant success. – She is but newly arrived, and has not as yet had time sufficient to exhibit her charms in that extensive line, that must gain her universal approbation, I could almost say preference, where I not restrained by the old adage, 'every eye makes a beauty' – Who could think such an original dearly purchased at the price of five guineas.

Mrs. G–, at Mrs. L–es. No. 9, *Wardour-street.*

Let glittering meteors dart along the skies,
And for a moment flash in human eyes,
Here milder radiance may be daily seen,
Reflect its influence from the charming Green.

To attempt a degree of praise that could approach the merit of this enchanting girl, would only expose us to the fate of Phaeton; and our want of skill might prove prejudicial to her, which is by no means our wish. For who can, with the most unerring knowledge of the English tongue, succeed in conveying an adequate idea of the yet, scarcely ripened charms of a lass of eighteen; whose auburn tresses serve only as a foil to the loveliest

skin that ever nature put the finishing hand to:
– or who can find language sufficiently expressive
to represent those swelling orbs, whose velvet
softness is exceeded only by the solidity of their
texture, where the capillary veins in meandering
folds, conveys the azure tide, to and from the
heart with a warmth that communicates itself to
the whole frame; and excites such commotions as
claim the highest approbation of those who have
the happiness of participating in her feelings; and
this any gentleman may do for two guineas, the
moderate price of a single *tete-a tete*: a night will
be considered cheap at twice the sum.

Mrs. Pi–ce, No. 19, *St. George's Row, Apollo Gardens.*

This lovely girl can post a power of charms,
When love entwines her in her lover's arms.

This girl at present possesses every requisite to
form the good, the agreeable bed-fellow. She is
still in her teens, with fine dark eyes and hair,

her mouth opens to display a regular set of teeth; pretty panting bubbies which do not require to be pressed or deformed by that very unnecessary covering, the stays; in bed she will twine and twist, sigh and murmur, pant and glow with unfeigned emotions, and never be tired of love's game, whilst the *blind boy* can find the way *in*, perfect good nature is predominant in all the features of this female, and her behaviour displays so much artless simplicity, that she never fails to win the affections of her male visitors; all the joys that is in the power of love to give, from her may be expected, for which a moderate computation satisfies her, as she is by no means mercenary.

Mifs –, No. 44, *Newman-street, Oxford Street.*

Here stop your wandering steps, thou
  am'rous youth,
Behold this emblem of untainted truth;
Here eyes declare the secret flame within,
Her lovely form would tempt a saint to sin.

This *petite* belle has not yet attained her sixteenth year; and, to make amends for her deficiency of height, she is elegantly formed, nor does she lack beauty. Her sparkling eyes would warm an anchorite. Her hair is beautifully fair: and her liveliness in conversation renders her a most agreeable companion. Two guineas will bring you better acquainted with this charmer; nor will you have cause for disagreeable reflections from her acquaintance.

Mrs. Mac–tney, *Great Titchfield-ſtreet.*

Come you young rascal, leave off crying,
I will whip you while the rod will last!
I will! I will! You're always lying,
I will whip you for all offences past.

There is nothing gives me so much pride
Than such amusement with a youth!
To whip! whip! his bold backside,
When he tells lies, instead of truth!

Plunge and caper! roar and cry!
I have you now within my power!
No kind protector now is nigh,
Thro' life I'll make you bless this hour,
And bless this hand that holds the rod!
And kiss it with a fervor sweet!
And think yourself a demi-god!
While tasting the delicious treat!

Keep down your legs, let go my hand,
Let, let your breeches remain down,
This efficacious reprimand,
Shall make you the best boy in town.

Here a very genteel figure unites with a beautiful
countenance, heightened with a lovely fair
complexion, and very expressive blue eyes; this
lady, who is about twenty-five years, appears
conscious of her own consequence, charms and
attractions, and often gives herself some airs that
were better laid aside, for pride and haughtiness in
the finest woman cannot fail of being disagreeable
it is true she has a very genteel set of visitors,
who pay proper attention to her extraordinary
agreements, and she will not suffer a plebeian or

a tradesmen to be introduced to her. She was married very young to an officer, who died a very short time after; she then took a house and followed the mantua-making business; as she let lodgings, a Russian gentleman took her first floor; her first appearance in public life happened thus: at that time a niece of hers, a girl about thirteen, lived with her as an apprentice, she being exceeding lazy and wicked, her aunt used to smart her bum very often with the birch rod; one day she sent her to get change for a guinea, Miss, after staying a long while came at last, and with a most innocent air, told her aunt, she had lost in the way half a guinea out of the change, the other believed her; two or three days after, curiosity prompted her to look into her niece's box, there she found a number of new toys, particularly a large doll, which could not cost less than five shillings; she came down instantly, called her niece and asked her with what money she had bought all the toys she had just seen in her box, the girl at first said it was given to her, but soon by threats confessed that she bought them with the *lost* half guinea; the aunt flew into a violent passion, sent the maid immediately for a birch broom, and picked out of it about two dozen of the best and greenest twigs; she was just tying them up with a ribbon when the Russian gentleman entered; she acquainted him with the whole affair, and found him a great advocate for the punishment she was going to inflict on her niece. She then left him in the front parlour, and retired into a back one with the young minx, and, for near a quarter of an hour, flogged her like an enraged school-mistress; after she had done, she returned into the parlour where she had left the gentleman, who had seen the whole of the transaction through key-hole; the conversation turned on the necessity of correcting children; the Russian, who was a most beautiful man, at last fixing his eyes on her beautiful bosom, which, from the exertion of the rod and the passion she was in, was still heaving, and paying her many compliments, told her how happy he would be to be a nephew of hers, and to be served just as she had her niece; at first she did not understand him, but recollecting herself, and having often heard of gentlemen who take a delight in being whipped by women, she listened to him and on his enforcing his *argument* with a five pound bank note, she made a new rod, and whipt him till he was completely gratified. All the time he lived in the house, she used to go up to his bed-chamber, about eleven o'clock dressed, according to his desire, in a white *deshabillé*, with a black hat adorned with six large white ostrich feathers, her hair dressed in the extreme of fashion, and a beautiful bouquet in her bosom of a most enormous size, bought that very morning at Covent Garden, then she would whip him with a large bundle of new birch for not getting up sooner, with a severity scarce credible, the comedy would then finish by his plunging into the *Gulph of Venus*, raising her soul to extatic bliss, and giving her such a treat of voluptuous enjoyment, such a feast of amorous delight as to convince her of the *magic* of a birch rod. It is supposed that for the short time she lived with that gentleman she got near £500 from him; on

his leaving London, having acquired a propensity
for the birch discipline, she bought a genteel day
school for young ladies near town, which she kept
a few years with much credit, and by the frequent
and severe whippings she gave to her scholars, she
forwarded them in their learning in such a manner
as to give utmost satisfaction to all parents.

Mrs. M– has now with her two young beautiful
tits, one about fifteen and the other sixteen, who
are always dressed in frocks like school girls; a
certain foreign nobleman often visits her, and
being fond of the game of school mistress, to
please him, she generally assumes the character
of a governess, and
makes the young
misses read to her; on
their not reading to
her satisfaction, she
takes up the young
naughty girls on her
lap, one after another,
and whips them well
with a good birch rod,
to the great delight of
the nobleman, who

is soon served in the same manner by one of the *naughty* girls. No one can be admitted into her house without being first introduced.

Mifs H–r–y, No. 16, *Phœnix street, Soho.*

Whisper'd plaints; and wanton wiles;
Speeches soft, and soothing smiles,
Teeth imprinted, tell-tale kisses,
Intermix with all my kisses.

This young lady is possessed of considerable charms, which she endeavours to set off to the best advantage; but good friends is not the lot of every one, even if the deserve them. If unaffected good nature, natural blooming complexion, sparkling black eyes, expressive of deep penetration, a regular set of ivory teeth, with tresses flowing in tempting ringlets down her back are entitled to recommendation, this wanton and lovely Cyprian fair one can with justice boast to an eminent degree of those desirable accomplishments. Report says, she has been but a few months in public practice, which from good authority, we are given to understand is but Six. She is frequently to be met with at the original Thirteen Cantons, in King Street, Soho. Any gentleman desirous of visiting this delicate girl, may rest perfectly satisfied of experiencing, not only a polite reception, but infinite pleasure in the embraces of this loving and amorous female. One guinea for one night's repose will not be thought over much. Nineteen years is the age of this nymph.

Mifs W–ll–m's, No. 9, *Upper Newman-street, Middlesex Hospital.*

Balmy sweetness ever flowing
From those ruby lips distil,
Roses on thy cheeks are blowing,
And thy voice like music thrills.

In the memoirs of this wanton female, we present our readers with a tall, genteel girl, very pretty face, fair complexion, and desirable auburn coloured ringlets, which flow in tempting curls across a delicately white breast; her beautiful set of teeth, add considerably to her angelic appearance, which generally commands admiration from most of her visitors: her disposition is peculiarly amorous and engaging, assisted with a brilliant tell-tale and love sparkling eye. What is a great recommendation to this lovely Cyprian nymph is her vocal abilities, which may with truth be said to be of no inconsiderable power; her musical skill certainly is of great promise and we are firmly persuaded, any gentleman who takes the trouble of visiting this divine siren will be fully satisfied in the above assertion. She is frequently to be noticed in the green boxes of the theatres, where by her natural good temper she gains many genteel admirers. She is reported to be an incomparable and enchanting bedfellow, and has a peculiar art in raising them that fall, and bringing the dead to life. Two pounds two shillings is the price of admission to enter her unfurnished parlour, which we are convinced is at a moment's notice ready for the reception of any gentleman. Twenty years is this lady's age.

❧❧❧❧❧❧❧❧❧❧❧❧❧❧❧❧❧❧❧❧❧❧❧❧❧

SELECTIONS

FROM

EARLIER EDITIONS

OF THE

Harris's List

1761–1791

———

'GOOD-NATURED GIRLS'

Jenny Nelson, *St. Martin's Lane.*

Ajolly smart wench, a good companion at table; but particularly joyous in bed; there are few whores to be found so generous as she is, often restoring the money when she likes her man; but she drinks damnably, and is then too apt to be saucy. (1761)

Miss Betsy Clarke, 11 *Stephen St., Rathbone Place.*

Hope with a gaudy prospect feeds the eye,
Sooths every sense, does with each wish
      comply,
But false enjoyment the kind guide destroys,
We lose the passion in the treacherous joys

Enjoyment is the most exquisite of human pleasures; ah! What a pity it is so short in duration. Nature wound up to the highest pitch, after striking twelve immediately descends to poor solitary one: these are the restrictions that naturally arise on enjoying Betsy. Though she is but little, she is an epitome of delight, a quintessence of joy, which by the most endearing chemistry, give all spirit, and unite in small compass the efficacy of a much larger bulk. Her lovely fair tresses and elegant countenance beat alarms to love; but we attack only to fall in the breach, and lament that the luscious conflict is so soon ended. The common destroyer of beauty has made a few dells on the face of this fair Jewess, but a pair of pretty dimples makes ample amends, and quite over-balances these trifling imperfections; she has been in life not more than six months, and expects, if she calls any man a friend, to receive two guineas the first visit. (1788)

Mrs. Whiting, alias Sketch, *Bury Street, St. James'.*

This young lady is rather too short; though she makes ample amends for that deficiency in her complexion, which is quite clear and fine. Her figure on the whole is genteel. Her appearance in loose attire is enchanting; such as would almost provoke old age, or even impotence, to make an effort of plunging in the circle of bliss. (1761)

The Full-Figured

Miss Clicamp, 2, *York St.*, *Middlesex Hospital.*

Strange it is, but not less strange than true, that Englishmen in general have a great itch for variety; and according to our promissory note in the preface, we here present them with one of the finest, fattest figures as fully finished for fun and frolick as fertile fancy ever formed; fraught with every melting charm that can be found in the field of Venus, fortunate for the true lovers of fat, should fate throw them into the possession of such full grown beauties. (1788)

Miss Jordan, No. 20, *Little Wild Street.*

As a remarkable woman, we could not pass over this lady, for she is an absolute curiosity, weighing, at least seventeen or eighteen stone, and considering that this is no light weight to carry, she is very nimble—we must confess we should be very loath to trust ourselves with her in bed lest we should be overlaid, or that she should chuse to place herself in a *particular posture*, and we should be that way smothered; she is very fair, and has a face somewhat resembling a full moon, she is always neat and clean in her dress, and is said to have a particular *natural curiosity*, equally remarkable with her person, either of which are open to the inspection of the curious on reasonable terms. (1779)

Red-Heads

Miss Nunn, 15 *Compton Street.*

The golden locks that shade those killing eyes,
In wanton folds embrace her snowy neck;
The yellow mantle fixt between the thighs
With envious ringlets Venus's altar deck

This lewd piece of gigantic love (being full six feet high) has figured away in a very prosperous line these last nine months, nor does her amorous appetite seem in the least abated, she looks to be only about nineteen. If carroty locks create lewdness (as is believed by some) we need not wonder at this lasses fire, she is so amply stored with it both above and below; below its great use is immediately pointed out; for did not this impervious armour shade the font of life, the battered premises would often want repairing, now it stands unshocked at the fierce attacks. During your engagement with this piece of wanton fire, you should be particularly cautious just at the coming in of the heat, not to suffer her teeth to come in contact with any very tender part, we have known a case where a gentleman lost part of his tongue upon the occasion. As she is in good keeping by a nobleman of Grosvenor Square, you can not value her favours at less than three guineas. (1791)

Bet Ellis, *Chandos Street.*

A little, diminutive, smirking, lecherous hussey, a very wart upon the crudities of Venus. She has some very odd tricks with her, which however, may be pleasing to those depraved appetites, who strive to improve upon the qualifications of nature; in a word 'tis her particular pleasure in the encounters of love, to claim that superiority which nature allotted to the man. Neither her teeth nor her legs are good, and by being red-haired, she emits an unsavoury effluvia, which alone is enough to damp the ardour of an elegant debauchee. (1761)

Don's Delight

Mrs. Br—s, 12 *Goodge St.*

Upon the bed she lays as she were slain
'Till his breath breathed life into her again

A collegian of the University of Cambridge engrosses this lady's attention all the night, that is out of term time; so that whoever wishes to enjoy her company must pay his visit early in the evening, which is the time her friend visits the coffee house. She is upon the whole a desirable piece, and considering her business is generally transacted on a coach, acquits herself as well as any of the train. As her customers are mostly flying visitors she does not expect more than half a guinea; especially as she encourages her hairdresser (one Burke) to occupy so much of her attention. (1789)

Hannah Dalton, *Swallow Street, Piccadilly.*

A strapping florid wench of St. Patrick's breed, rather too masculine for the delicacy required in a fine woman; but she has this to make up for any personal defects, that she has better sense, and received a much better education than most of her sort. Her father was butler to Trinity College, Dublin, whence she sucked milk from Alma mater. 'Tis reported, indeed that before she was 18 she sucked something else from every nipple in the university; she is an indifferent bedfellow; being most agreeable when over a bottle, and half drunk. (1761)

Lawyers' Lovers

Mrs. B—rdm—e, 3 *Little Chapel Street, Soho.*

> If Azure eyes and pouting lips
> If tempting cheeks and velvet tips
> Can move the lover to the game
> Here may he quench his amorous flame

This lady is as true a devotee to the deity of love as ever gambolled in his mother's train, compelled to fly from the tyranny of an ignorant sottish husband, her ill-fortune threw her into the hands of the most dangerous creature in society, who having nothing to fear from loss of character, has everything to hope from the weakness, misfortunes, and credulity of their wretched prey; I mean an unprincipled attorney. Unfortunately for poor Mary, she conceived a fondness for Mr. C— of Gray's Inn; who under the pretence of doing her justice, he instituted suits in several courts against her husband, and she blinded by her fondness, signed every paper tendered to her. Having satisfied his lust upon her, and his avarice (as far as possible) on her husband, to compleat his character, he then abandoned the fond, the too credulous fair. Though not blessed with what painters call a fine face, she has an agreeable pleasing countenance, and nature, as though conscious of her neglect above, has made ample amends on her parts below. She is tall in stature, well turned limbs, plump and round and is so zealous in her devotions, that we would advise none, but the most capable, to hazard an engagement. (1789)

Betsy Bentinck alais B—t—y, alias Stickland, alias Ucklersbury.

This woman is tall and well made; and may be justly termed a fine figure. Her legs are none of the best, for which reason her cloaths are made remarkably long. She is reported to have very little sensation, and that the largest man in England may draw her on like a jack-boot. Her skin is bad, her mouth wide, and her eyes rather heavy than languishing. She can put on a pleasing countenance when she pleases, which is seldom. She was once in Jamaica, in the service of a noble admiral's lady, against whom she appeared as a witness in a remarkable case of adultery, in which her master was plaintiff, and a captain of a man of war defendant. The latter she charges with having debauched her. An attorney's clerk in Furnival's Inn kept her for some time, upon the slender diet of bread, cheese and small beer; but has lately exchanged him for a fat grocer in the city, who gives her a scanty pittance, which she increases by plying near the Change, Leadenhall Street and some bye places, as a rose never blown on. (1761)

CLERGYMEN'S BELLES

Miss Ross, 8 *Little Ryder Street*, *St. James'*.

This lady's complexion is dark, as well as her eyes and hair. Her teeth are regular and white. She is very affable and engaging in her disposition, and calls forth all her powers to give delight, with uncommon success; her age is eighteen, and her entrance into life is about eight months. She is a great dreamer, and frequently entertains her friends with her reveries, which are generally romantic and whimsical. She has been for sometime wavering with respect to religion, and a certain Methodist preacher has taken great pains to make a convert of her, but a roman catholic priest, who visits her *a la sourdine*, countermines in the evening all his rival's operations in the morning; so that between Methodism and Popery, she is a skiff upon the ocean tossed, and can not find a safe port to anchor in. She is however, pretty well known to be in keeping by a clergyman who is dotingly fond of her, and in whose absence only is she come-at-able, at the moderate price of two or three guineas. (1791)

Sally Cummins, *Charles Street, Westminster.*

A bluish eyed comely lass, but too much indebted to art for her complexion. She talks French, and sings agreeably, and in her cups is very religious, when you should find her to be a most bigoted Papist. She is descended of a genteel family in Wiltshire, and was bred up in a nunnery in France. How she came among the sisters of carnality, no body knows. She positively denies her having been debauched by a friar. (1761)

ARMY AMOURS

Polly Armstrong, *Warwick Street, Golden-Square.*

This young lady was formerly a milliner, in which capacity she was debauched by a young officer of the guards; and leaving off her business

(of which she had never very much) for some time lived with him on bare subsistence; but finding lieutenants pay but bad support for two, he mustered up five guineas and put her away of doing for herself. She accordingly began to see company, as the phrase is, and soon became a girl of reputation. The small-pox, which she has had within these two years, has altered her, but still she is a desirable girl, and a man need not be very hungry to make a love meal upon her. (1761)

Miss Smith, *Bridges Street*.

This dear little devil is fair, agreeable and young, being no more than twenty. Several connoisseurs in the profession have given us a satisfactory account of the various ways she contrives to please her cull. Being well acquainted with her behaviour, she may depend on being introduced into the best of company— Some of the officers of the Plessey Indiamen are greatly beholden to her for late *eminent services*, which they will have occasion to remember to they get to the Indies, or even, perhaps, till they come back again. (1764)

Nelly Anderson, *Dean Street Soho.*

A squat, swarthy, round faced wench, from the other side of the Tweed. She has of late seldom been in London, but during the winter, having kept her summer residence at the different camps, being a particular admirer of red coats. It is to this company that we must attribute her swearing, drinking, and talking bawdy, which she does with as good grace as any of the bunters of Drury-Lane. (1761)

BUXOM

Miss Brown, 14 *Old Compton Street, Soho.*

This pretty bit of luscious stuff is not above nineteen; she is remarkably full breasted of her age. It is said that a certain gentleman whose name she now goes by, was so enamoured with her pouting orbs, which before they attained their present extent, he compared to two poached eggs in fine preservation, that he desired to cover them with two bank notes of twenty pounds each, whenever he regaled himself with such a luxuriant banquet; her complexion is very fair, her hair light, and her eyes wantonly brilliant, inclinable to a fine blue. Her temper is affable and complaisant; and though she is well known to be one of us, yet, she is very choice of her company. However a couple of guineas will have its due influence, if properly presented. (1791)

Mrs. Wood, 3 *Lisle St., Leicester Fields.*

Oh! That deceit should steal such gentle
     shapes,
And with a virtuous vizard hide deep vice

Men's palates are as various as their faces, and like a good ordinary we would offer up a dish for every palate. In the time of the ancient Romans we are told that the fat paps of the sow were held a great dainty. For those that have a relish for such a repast we recommend Mrs. Wood, and can assure them such paps as she possesses are seldom to be met with. She keeps the house, and is wife to Squire P–'s coachman, late of the stables, Bolton street; her front is well-brazen'd; her face is continually upon the full grin, and as for talking bawdy, swearing, or bare fac'd indecency, she could vie with the ancient Messelina of Rome; she dispenses her favours for any sum to one whose arms are sufficiently long to embrace her, and may do now, but in the dog days must be intolerable. (1788)

SPIRITED SPARKS

Miss Hussey, at *Mrs. Giffard's, Martlet Court, Covent Garden.*

Behold a ripe and melting maid
Bound 'prentice to the wanton trade

This lady's features are very agreeable and tolerably
regular, which, with a plump and pleasing figure,
and lovely breasts, make her, though a woman, the
father of lust, which she begetteth on every eye
that sees her. She has brown hair, is young and of
the middle size; and when only some of the senses
are to be gratified, she can not fail of pleasing.

Sometimes she takes a cup too much, and then
woe be to them that fall under her displeasure
– all the mischievous weapons she can lay her
hand on are sure to be thrown at the culprits
heads, and happy if they escape unhurt!

*Ye Gods! What havock doth the –bottle make
'mongst woman kind!* (1773)

———————————————

Miss Randall, No. 8, *Nag's Head Court, Drury Lane.*

Buxom Frolic, Gay and Free

A wild, airy, thoughtless girl, about twenty, of
an honest well-meaning disposition, and no
one's enemy but her own; has a fair complexion;

grey eyes and a good leg; she bears an excellent character for her spirited behaviour, during her *amorous exertions*. But she is too fond of strong waters to be quite agreeable, a fault which a great majority of the sisterhood are guilty of, though we rather hope from habit than inclination. (1779)

LADIES OF EXPERIENCE

Mrs. Griffin, near *Union Stairs, Wapping*.

This comely woman, about forty, and boasts she can give more pleasure than a dozen raw girls. Indeed she has acquired great experience, in the course of twenty years study in natural philosophy at the university of Portsmouth, where she was long the ornament of the back of the point. She is perfectly mistress of all her actions and can proceed regularly from the dart of her tongue, and the soft tickle of her hand, to the ecstatic squeeze of her thighs; the enchanting twine of her legs; the elaborate suction of her lower lips, and the melting flood of delight with which she constantly bedews the mossy root of the tree of life, and washes the testimonies of manhood; tho' past her meridian she is still agreeable; her eyes are black as well as her hair, of which she has an abundance both above and below, her breasts are large but not flabby, and her skin is fair. Five shillings is her price, and she earns it with great industry; but if her lover seems capable of prolonging the delicious banquet, and is remarkably well provided, she will abate weight for inches. Her chief and best customers are sea officers, whom she particularly likes, as they do not stay long at home, and always return fraught with love and presents. (1788)

Mrs. Hamblin, No. 1, *Naked-Boy Court, near the New Church, Strand.*

The plaister'd nymph returns the kiss,
Like Thisby, through a wall

The *young* lady in question, is not above *fifty-six*, and according to her own confession has been a *votary* to *pleasure* these thirty years, she wears a substantial *mask* upon her face, and is rather short. We should not have introduced her here, but that on account of her long experience and extensive practice, we know that she must be particularly useful to *elderly* gentlemen, who are very *nice* in having their linen got up. (1779)

Kitty Buckley, *Poland Street.*

This lady has been at the service of every man that has a mind to her, from her thirteenth year. Her mamma was a midwife in Ireland, from which country Miss Buckley came. No woman was ever more hackney'd from the lord to the porter; Turks, Jews, Papists; every sect, and every country have tasted her sweet body. She is really an elegant figure, and has a charming sweetness in her countenance; but she is as wicked as a devil, and as extravagant as Cleopatra. She is generally three times a year in the bailiff's hands, but still makes a figure. She is now descending into the vale of years, being at least five and thirty; and is reported to have ruined twenty keepers. (1761)

FOREIGN BEAUTIES

Mrs. Lowes, *Upper Charlotte Street, Rathbone Place.*

Sure nature cast one in her softest mould
All mild and gentle, never made to scold

West Indies gave birth to this daughter of Momus by Venus; the warmth of the clime brought the charming girl's feelings to maturity at an early period, and a gentleman, whose name she assumes, first trod down Hymen's fence, and made her a perfect woman; but the natural warmth of her constitution soon compelled her to seek variety in our great mart; she therefore left her good friend, and now presents the world with a sweet cheerful disposition, fine dark hair, and eyes of the same friendly hue; fine teeth, is short and plump, and we have not had her above eighteenth months; she expects three guineas for a whole night, but if you make a short visit, one pound one shilling is the least. (1788)

———————————————

Miss Townsend, 15 *Stevens Street,*
Rathbone Place.

The use of the needle first fired this lady's imagination with the use of a certain pin. She passed two years before her public entrance into life at a milliner's in the town of Boston in America. The discourse between the experienced matrons in that dear initiating school, so warmed her naturally wanton heart, that they fell an easy snare to the first male trap, that fell in her way. Her god fortune soon threw her into the arms of an indulgent keeper, with whom she lived for some time, both before and since they have arrived in this country, the cause of her leaving him we are not acquainted with; suffice to say we are certain she refuses no visitors, that will afford a couple of guineas and a bottle. She is now bordering on nineteen. (1789)

PERVERSIONS

Nancy Burroughs, near the *Devil's Gap, Drury Lane.*

Very impudent and very ugly; chiefly a dealer
with old fellows. It is reported that she uses
more birch rods in a week than Westminster
school in a twelvemonth. In a word, this lady
will condescend to oblige her companion in
whatsoever way he likes, if she is but sure of
being well paid for it. (1761)

Betsy Miles, at a *Cabinet maker's Old Street, Clerkenwell.*

Which way you will and please you

Known in this quarter for her immense sized
breasts, which she alternately makes use of with
the rest of her parts, to indulge those who are
particularly fond of a certain amusement. She
is what you may call, at all; backwards and

forwards, are all equal to her, posteriors not excepted, nay indeed, by her own account she has most pleasure in the latter. Very fit for a foreign Macaroni – entrance at the front door tolerably reasonable, but nothing less than two pound for the back way. As her person has nothing remarkable one way or the other, we shall leave her for those of the Italian gusto. (1773)

Miss Bland, *Wardour Street, Soho.*

This is a gay volatile girl; very genteel in her person; and has an extraordinary titillation in all her members; which she is very fond of increasing, by making use of provocatives for that purpose such as pullets, pigs, veal, new-laid eggs, oysters, crabs, prawns, eringoes, electuaries, &c. &c. – She

is reported to have a kind of savage joy in her embraces, and sometimes leaves the marks of her penetrating teeth on her paramour's cheeks. (1764)

Miss H—lsb—ry, No.14, *Goodge Street.*

This Pleasant vineyard is well stor'd with fruit,
And many a plant here has taken root.

This young lady is finely made, with a prepossessing countenance, expressive dark eyes, fine hands and arms, and proclaims the woman of consequence fit for the first rate company, into which she is often introduced. Nevertheless, having got the better of that *mauvaise houte,* with which our ladies are so much accused, with what reason it is difficult to say, she is careless about her expressions and neither shudders at a double entendre, or trembles at a single entendre: in fine, she may, in more senses than one, be pronounced a great linguist. A velvet salute of this kind, had nearly disgusted Lord L—; but having got over the first impression, he found that her tongue was attuned to more airs than one; but she never admits either of her mouths to be play'd with for less than two guineas. She appears very genteel, and is supposed to be in keeping by a Mr. Grace of Duke Street, St. James. (1789)

Poxed!

Miss Young, No. 6, *Cumberland Court or Turk's Head Bagnio, Bridge's Street.*

Miss Young is an adopted *child* to the bawd, who keeps, or more properly speaking, is kept by the above mentioned houses, and is so very fond of cutting a *figure*, that in a hired tawdry silk gown, she will fancy herself a woman of the first quality.

We mentioned her in the last list as tolerably handsome, but of a disposition mercenary, almost beyond example, her beauty is now vanished, but her avarice remains, and what is worse, she has very lately had the folly and wickedness to leave a certain hospital, before the cure of a certain distemper which she had was completed, and has thrown her contaminated carcass on the town again, for which we hold her inexcusable, and which was our only reason for repeating her name, that her company might be avoided, and that she might be held in the infamous light she so justly deserves for her willful villainy. (1779)

Sally Robinson, *Maiden Lane.*

The origin of this lady is a little obscure, but she sold sausages about the streets till above fifteen years old, when the celebrated Mrs. Cole had a casual sight of her maidenhead for thirty guineas; out of which she generously made Sall a present of five shillings, to cure her of the clap, which she got from her deflowerer. She is a tall, fat girl, but not ungenteel, nor her face disagreeable; but she is as mercenary as the devil, which lessens all her other good qualities (1761)

Also from Tempus:

For the full story of *The Harris's List*...

The Covent Garden Ladies
Pimp General Jack & the Extraordinary Story of Harris's List
HALLIE RUBENHOLD
£9.99
978 07524 3739 2

'Has all the atmosphere and edge of a good novel...
magnificent'
Frances Wilson, author of *The Courtesan's Revenge*

'Scrupulously researched and cleverly structured... as lewd as
goats and monkeys'
The Daily Telegraph

'A compelling and ingenious book... Rubenhold proves herself
both a keen researcher and a writer who understands narrative
tension'
The Independent on Sunday

'Sex toys, porn... forget Ann Summers, Miss Love was at it 250
years ago'
The Times

TEMPUS – REVEALING HISTORY

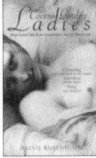

Quacks Fakers and Charlatans in Medicine
ROY PORTER

'A delightful book' *The Daily Telegraph*

'Hugely entertaining' *BBC History Magazine*

£12.99   0 7524 2590 0

The Tudors
RICHARD REX

'Up-to-date, readable and reliable. The best introduction to England's most important dynasty' *David Starkey*

'Vivid, entertaining... quite simply the best short introduction' *Eamon Duffy*

'Told with enviable narrative skill... a delight for any reader' *THES*

£9.99   0 7524 3333 4

The Kings & Queens of England
MARK ORMROD

'Of the numerous books on the kings and queens of England, this is the best'
Alison Weir

£9.99   0 7524 2598 6

The Covent Garden Ladies
Pimp General Jack & the Extraordinary Story of Harris's List
HALLIE RUBENHOLD

'Sex toys, porn... forget Ann Summers, Miss Love was at it 250 years ago' *The Times*

'Compelling' *The Independent on Sunday*

'Marvellous' *Leonie Frieda*

'Filthy' *The Guardian*

£9.99   0 7524 3739 9

Okinawa 1945
GEORGE FEIFER

'A great book... Feifer's account of the three sides and their experiences far surpasses most books about war'
Stephen Ambrose

£17.99   0 7524 3324 5

Tommy Goes To War
MALCOLM BROWN

'A remarkably vivid and frank account of the British soldier in the trenches'
Max Arthur

'The fury, fear, mud, blood, boredom and bravery that made up life on the Western Front are vividly presented and illustrated'
The Sunday Telegraph

£12.99   0 7524 2980 4

Ace of Spies The True Story of Sidney Reilly
ANDREW COOK

'The most definitive biography of the spying ace yet written... both a compelling narrative and a myth-shattering *tour de force*'
Simon Sebag Montefiore

'The absolute last word on the subject' *Nigel West*

'Makes poor 007 look like a bit of a wuss'
The Mail on Sunday

£12.99   0 7524 2959 0

Sex Crimes
From Renaissance to Enlightenment
W.M. NAPHY

'Wonderfully scandalous' *Diarmaid MacCulloch*

'A model of pin-sharp scholarship' *The Guardian*

£10.99   0 7524 2977 9

If you are interested in purchasing other books published by Tempus, or in case you have difficulty finding any Tempus books in your local bookshop, you can also place orders directly through our website

www.tempus-publishing.com